ILLUSTRATED COLOR GUIDE TO HEALTHFUL YOGA

BELL PUBLISHING COMPANY • NEW YORK

Copyright © MCMLXXIII, LXXIV by Marshall Cavendish Ltd.
Library of Congress Catalog Card Number: 75-24606
All rights reserved.
This edition is published by Bell Publishing Company
a division of Crown Publishers, Inc.
by arrangement with Marshall Cavendish Ltd.
a b c d e f g h
Manufactured in the United States of America

About this book . . . .

Unisex Yoga is a unique book. A comprehensive course, designed by Lilian K. Donat, one of Britain's most experienced and respected teachers, it gives you full instructions and step by step colour photographs to enable you to master all the basic yoga exercises and postures. Yoga has many paths, leading to the ultimate goal of poise, grace, peace of mind, and complete harmony with the world. One of these paths concentrates on creating a graceful, supple and totally alive body, and that is the aim of this book.

Yoga is for everyone — all these exercises are suitable for both men and women, and they are ideal for couples who want to learn yoga together. In a matter of weeks, you will feel more alive — your senses will be keener, and your mind alert and clear. You will feel more relaxed and tolerant, and far better able to cope with the strains and stresses of modern life. The main course consists of 20 basic lessons, and we have also included two valuable extras — a short course in the breathing techniques so essential to really good health, and a beautiful sequence called Sun Worship. This is a special self-contained set of exercises for you to enjoy as a pleasant change once you can do the basic postures.

Although this *Unisex Yoga* course is designed so that it can be completed in 20 weeks, this is a minimum time. It is flexible enough so that you can progress at your own pace, and you do not have to feel harassed at the idea of keeping up with a large class, which might not be suitable for your personal rhythm of development. The book is your own teacher, and you can practise in the privacy of your own home. Yoga develops your individual resources, which is a genuinely exciting experience, and if you are learning with someone else, you will also contribute to their development, as well as your own. Life takes on a completely new dimension as you become integrated with the world, and with yourself.

Lesson 1

"I'm sure it's good for you, but I'll never be able to do it." That is the reaction of most people to the idea of beginning yoga. They are unaware of the facts.

Yoga does not involve painful or acrobatic contortions. There are no exhausting exercises to endure, no laborious schedules to maintain. There is no magical mysticism.

The secret of yoga lies in creating and conserving energy, not in dissipating it. Rather than rippling biceps and bulging thighs, with yoga you develop slender, responsive muscles and a supple, mobile body. The exercises apply delicate pressures, persuading and stretching, stimulating glands and circulation, encouraging deep and relaxing breathing.

Yoga is a total form of physical and mental control. It is a system of self-renewal. Developed thousands of years ago in India to supreme precision, it has many layers of involvement and can answer many different needs. It can be the means of acquiring a slim, supple and healthy body. It can be the way to achieve inner tranquility. And, for a dedicated few, it is the path to great spiritual attainment.

It is an essential part of yoga that the mind and body are inseparable—that the well-being of one is interdependent with the other. The aim of hatha yoga, the physical system of yoga, is to achieve balance, to achieve harmony between the body and the mind.

This course of yoga has been specifically designed to enable men and women to become physically fit and relaxed. Each practice session will take only 30 minutes, a short period of each day that will become an integral part of your life. The exercises will invigorate your body and refresh your mind. They will make you better able to cope with the physical and mental demands which are made upon you.

In practice, hatha yoga is a system of exercises quite unlike any other—although many of the discoveries of yoga teachers have been borrowed and incorporated into other exercise programmes. You will finish each yoga session fresher and more alert than when you started. What other concentrated form of exercise could prepare you so well for a hard day's work?

Yoga will spread a sense of relaxation and well-being into your daily life. Your muscles will be firmer and your joints

looser. Your posture will be excellent and your shape beautiful. Yoga will make you look better and feel better.

All this is without effort. It is a cardinal rule of yoga that if you begin to strain as you do an exercise, you should stop. There is no need to force your body. It is enough to do each exercise only to the best of your own ability. And, even then, you will be amazed by the progress that will follow from regular, 30-minute practice sessions.

To gain the full benefit, try to make yoga a routine part of your day. First thing in the morning, before breakfast, is a good time to do yoga. If you can, choose a quiet and well-ventilated room and perform your postures on a folded blanket, a thick bath-towel or mat.

It is essential that your body be free when you do these exercises. If you wish to wear clothes be sure that they are not constricting.

Yoga should not be performed on a full stomach. It is advisable to wait for at least two hours after eating. A cool shower or bath to loosen up the body before starting is an advantage. A bath which is very hot, however, may encourage you to misjudge your suppleness.

Each session should begin and end with the relaxation pose. True relaxation is more difficult than you might think, so do not underestimate the importance of this pose.

Yoga postures are known as *asanas*, and there are two types, the static and the dynamic, although in some exercises they are combined. Static asanas are held for a certain length of time, while dynamic exercises require movement of either the whole body or parts of it. The movements in yoga are slow and graceful, without strain or hurry. Try to achieve a feeling of flowing transition as you move from one position to the next.

Breathing is very important in yoga. Take care to breathe slowly and deeply in the way directed for each particular asana. Most people use only part of their respiratory system. In yoga, unlike other physical exercises, the stress is laid on exhalation.

Remember that the time you devote to yoga is time devoted to the renewal of your mind and body. Now, relax and begin your first lesson. Do all these following exercises, as best you can every day for two weeks.

THE RELAXATION POSE

Lie on your back, feet slightly apart, arms at your sides, palms up and head and neck relaxed. Close your eyes. Put your tongue behind your lower teeth and relax your jaw. As always, breathe only through your nose. Try to relax your mind as well as your body. Remain like this for at least two minutes before and after each yoga session.

THE STICK POSE
Stretches and slims sides and waist and tones up back muscles As you do this exercise feel the stretch in your whole body

Straight Stretch
1. Lie on your back with your arms stretched over your head.
2. Inhale. Stretch your right arm and right leg as much as possible.

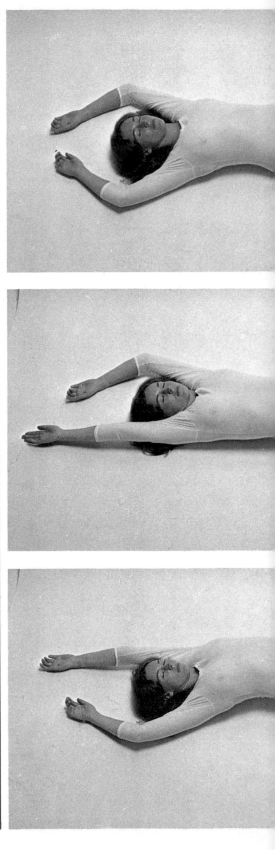

6

Hold to a mental count of five. Exhale and relax.

3. Repeat with your left arm and left leg.

Repeat three times on each side.

Diagonal Stretch (not illustrated)

Inhale. Stretch your right arm and left leg. Hold to a count of five. Exhale and relax.

Repeat with left arm and right leg. Repeat three times on each side.

ABDOMINAL BREATHING

Relaxes and calms
Essential for breath control of the abdominal muscles

1. Lie flat on your back with your hands at your sides. Inhale slowly to the mental count of four. Fill your abdomen with air.

2. Exhale slowly to the count of six or eight, contracting your abdomen as you do so.

Practise this slow and rhythmical breathing 10 times.

3. Bring the soles of your feet together and lower your knees. Hold your arms above your head with your elbows on the floor. In this posture you are forced to breath abdominally. Inhale to the count of six or eight. Repeat 10 times.

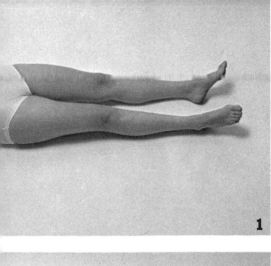

1

1

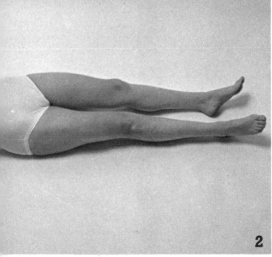

2

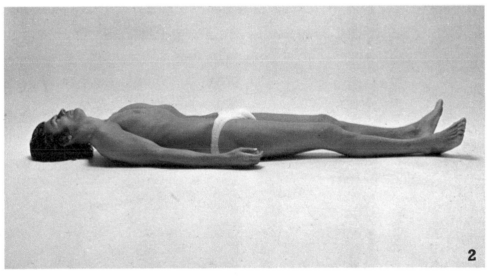

2

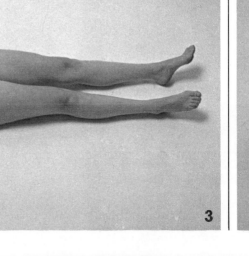

3

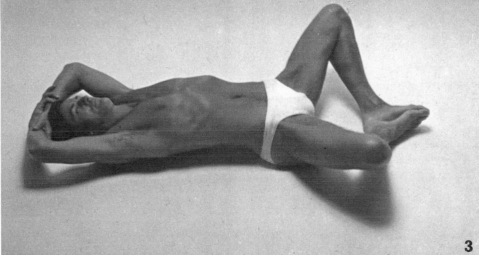

3

KNEE-BENDING
Stimulates the internal organs and counteracts hollow back

1. Lie on your back. Inhale. Bend your right knee and clasp your hands around it. Exhale and press your thigh against your chest. Repeat three times.
2. Inhale. Bend your left knee. Clasp your hands around it. Exhale and press your thigh against your chest. Repeat three times.
3. Bend both legs and clasp your hands around them. Inhale deeply. Press your thighs against your chest and exhale slowly. Repeat three times.

ROWING
Strengthens back and abdomen and shoulder muscles

1. Sit with your legs straight and your feet a few inches apart. Lean back. Bend your arms and make your hands into fists. Inhale.
2. Keeping your back straight, bend forward. Exhale and make rowing movement. Repeat six times.

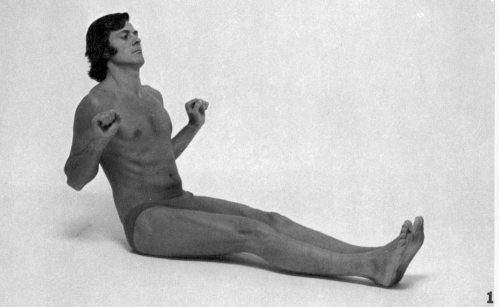

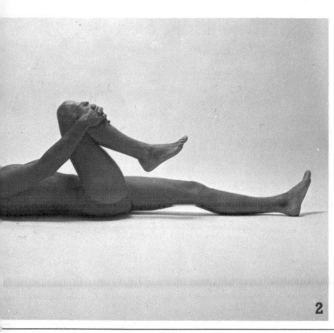

2

3

2

3

THE TWIST
Firms inner thighs, slims waist and strengthens spine

1. Sit with legs wide apart. Inhale and raise arms to shoulder height.
2. Twist your body from the waist and with your right hand try to touch your left big toe.
3. Stretch your left arm in line with your right arm and look back while exhaling slowly.
Straighten your body, then inhale and twist to the other side.
Repeat six times, moving slowly and smoothly from one side to the other.

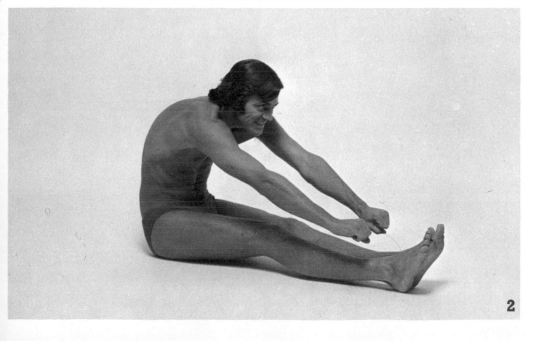

2

THE COBRA
Strengthens chin, neck and back muscles

1. Lie face down with your finger-tips parallel to the edge of your shoulders.
2. Put your forehead on the floor, feet resting on insteps and together.
3. Slowly push your chin forward.
4. Inhale and raise only your head and shoulders from the floor. Hold this pose for a mental count of 10. Exhale, put your chin back on the floor and slide back to your forehead.
Repeat once.

1

2

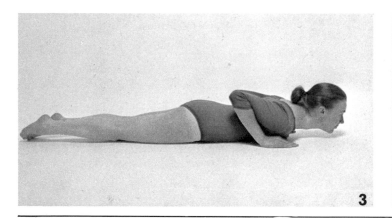

3

4

THE TREE
Develops poise, good balance and strengthens leg muscles

Put the sole of your left foot against your right inner thigh and as high as possible. Raise your arms to shoulder height. Focus your eyes on a point straight ahead.
Hold this posture for five breaths.

THE TRIANGLE
Slims waist and sides, strengthens spine and tones up muscles in the whole body

1. Stand with feet about three feet apart and arms outstretched at shoulder height.

2. Keeping your back straight, bend to the right, sliding your right hand down your leg. Bring your left arm over the top of your head so that its weight helps you to stretch a little further. Exhale as you go down. Come up slowly and inhale.

3. Bend to the other side.
Repeat three times on each side.

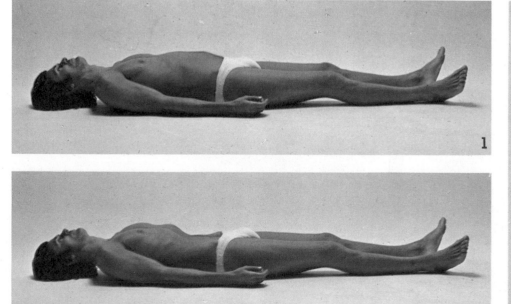

Lesson 2

How tense are you? It is quite easy to estimate—by becoming conscious of your movements and reactions you will soon realize how many unnecessary gestures you make with your hands, how often you clench your teeth, tap your feet, bite your nails, or wish to do so. Most of us are actually handicapped by habitual tension which lowers our vitality. It causes a draining of valuable energy, leaving us physically and emotionally depleted, unable to deal effectively with the tasks of everyday life.

A tense face, even with beautiful features, is never at its best, whereas a relaxed face is always attractive. Tension, not only harmful to yourself but also, in its own way, as infectious as chicken-pox, can be turned into a positive relaxed state of mind and body.

Although it is our natural birthright, relaxation often gets forgotten. But it can always be practised, even when you sit in a bus or have a lunch break. Relaxation is an integral part of hatha yoga and it is as important as the exercises themselves. Once you have found that you can relax, both in body and mind, you will be able to rid yourself of stress and strain in a very short time. By learning to tense and relax at will you will discover unexpected sources of inner strength and harmony.

The exercises which follow are a natural progression from those in the first session. Again it is a 30-minute programme, although this one is to be done only for one week. And again we begin by relaxing.

THE CROCODILE
Increases the suppleness of the spine and slims the waist
This exercise must be done slowly, smoothly and without interruption. The breath is held throughout.
1. Lie on the floor with arms raised to shoulder height and feet together.
2. Inhale and, keeping shoulders on the floor, turn your head to the left. Twisting your spine, turn your hips, legs and feet to the right.
3. In a continuous movement, and still holding your breath, twist in the opposite direction.
Return to original position. Exhale. Repeat three times.

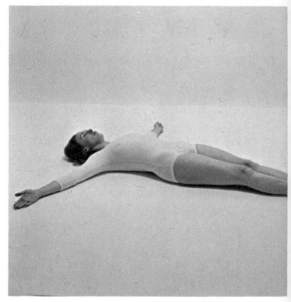

RELAXATION POSE
Lie on your back, feet slightly apart, arms at your sides, palms up and head and neck relaxed. Feel that all the little muscles in your cheeks relax. Imagine that a hand is slowly stroking your hair and relaxing your scalp. Breathe only through your nose. Try to relax your mind as well as your body. Remain like this for two minutes before and after each yoga session.

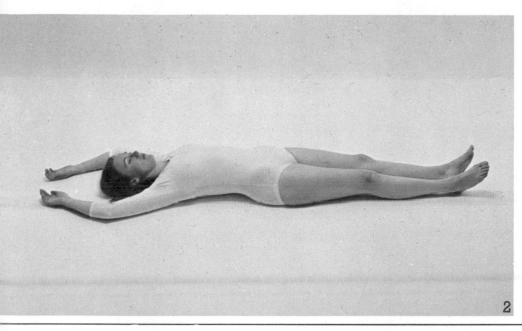

THE STICK POSE
Stretches and slims sides and waist, tones back, arm and leg muscles
1. Lie on your back with your arms stretched over your head. Inhale and stretch your whole body, including your arms and legs. Hold for a mental count of five.
2. Exhale, release stretch and contract all the muscles on either side of the spine, pressing the small of your back against the floor. Hold for the count of five.
Repeat three times.

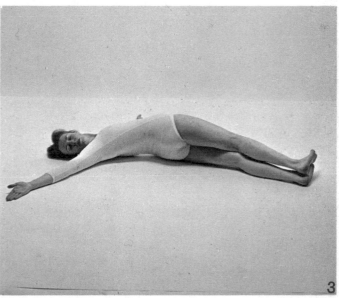

ABDOMINAL BREATHING
Relaxes and calms
Essential for breath control and control of the abdominal muscles
1. Lie flat on your back with your hands at your sides. Inhale slowly to the mental count of four.
Fill your abdomen with air.
2. Exhale slowly to the count of six or eight, contracting your abdomen as you do so.
Repeat four times.

THORACIC BREATHING
Increases the flexibility of the ribcage and the expansion of the lungs
1. Slightly tense your abdomen. Put your hands, with your fingers close together, on both sides of your ribcage. Inhale, filling your chest with air. Feel your ribs move sideways and outwards.
Exhale and feel your ribs move inwards and your fingertips join.
Repeat three times.

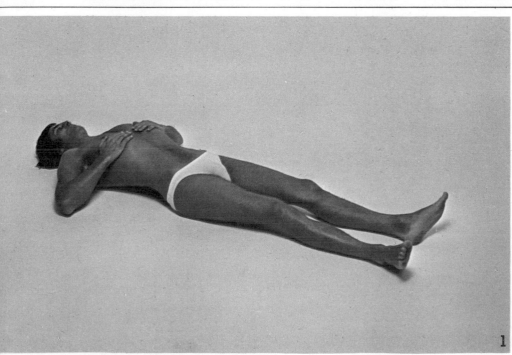

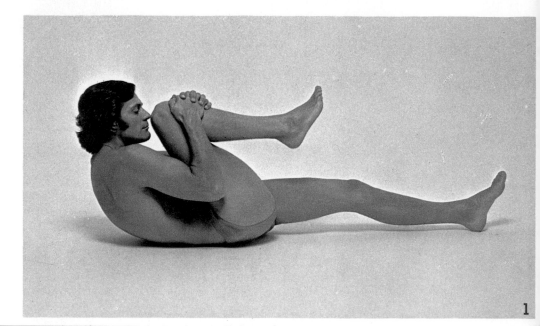

1

THE TWIST
Firms inner thighs, slims waist and strengthens spine
1. Sit with legs wide apart. Inhale and raise arms to shoulder height.
2. Twist your body from the waist and with your right hand try to touch your left big toe.
3. Stretch your left arm in line with your right arm and look back while exhaling slowly.
Straighten your body, then inhale and twist to the other side.
Repeat six times, moving slowly and smoothly from one side to the other.

1

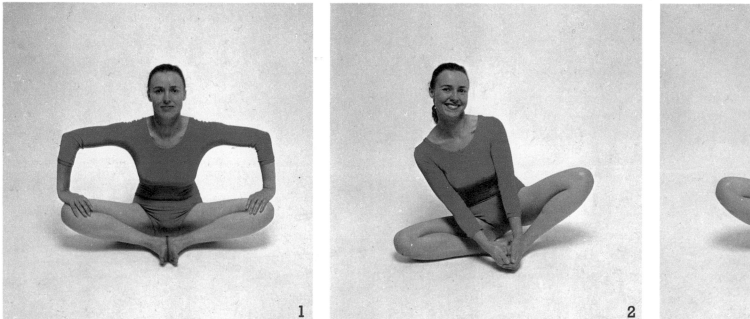

1

2

14

KNEE-BENDING – 2
Stimulates the internal organs, counteracts hollow back, stretches the muscles and nerves at of the back of the neck

1. Lie on your back. Bend your right knee and clasp your hands around it. Exhale and press your thigh against your chest, at the same time raising your head and bringing your nose to your knee. Hold for a count of three.

Inhale and relax, lowering head and shoulders to the ground.

Repeat three times with each leg.

2. Bend both legs and clasp your hands around them. Inhale deeply. Press your thighs against your chest and, at the same time, raise your head and shoulders and bring your nose to your knees. Exhale.

Repeat three times.

2

3

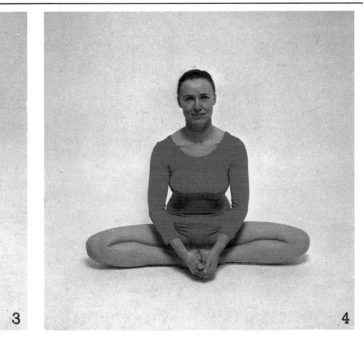

3

4

THE BUTTERFLY
Loosens the pelvic girdle and stretches and tones inner thigh muscles

1. Sit with the soles of your feet together and your heels as near to your body as possible.

Place your hands on your knees and very gently bounce them up and down 20 times. If you repeat this daily your knees will eventually come to the floor.

2-3. Clasp your feet with both hands and rock from side to side ten times.

4. Come back to original position.

THE COBRA -2
Strengthens chin, neck and back muscles

As you do this exercise imagine that you have the edge of a hoop against your back and that you are trying not to lose touch with it as you go up.

1. Lie face down, feet together and resting on insteps, with your fingertips parallel to the end of your shoulders and your forehead on the floor.

2. Slowly push your chin forward.

3. Inhale and raise your head, shoulders and chest by contracting the muscles at the back of your neck and upper part of your back. Hold for a count of five.

4. Raise your body a little higher and then, keeping your shoulders still, turn your face to the right and hold for a count of five. Turn your head to the left and, again, hold for a count of five. Facing forward again, exhale and come down slowly. Put your chin back on the floor and slide back to your forehead.

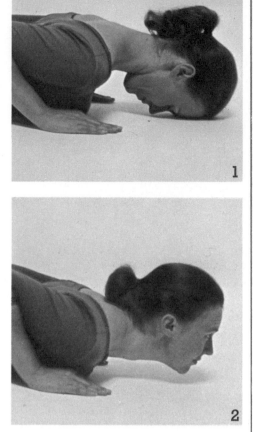

1

2

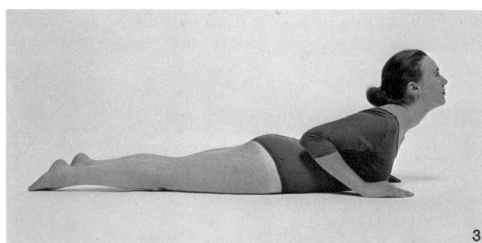

3

4

THE TIGHTROPE
Improves balance and concentration

Stretch your arms out and raise them to shoulder height. Slowly put one foot in front of the other, placing the heel against the toes. Walk forwards for at least ten steps. Then walk backward in the same way.

16

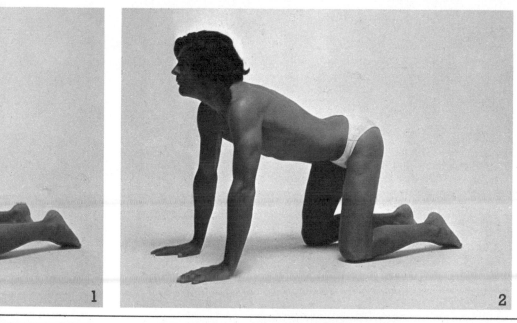

THE CAT
Counteracts hollow back, and strengthens abdominal muscles
1. With hands and knees parallel and apart, bend head down and look at your thighs. Do abdominal breathing six times, being careful to pull the abdomen in and up with each exhalation.
2. Inhale and arch your back inwards and raise your head.
Repeat five times.

1

2

THE TRIANGLE
Slims waist and sides, strengthens spine and tones up muscles in the whole body
Stand with feet about three feet apart and arms outstretched at shoulder height.
Keeping your back straight, bend to the right, sliding your right hand down your leg. Bring your left arm up over the top of your head so that its weight helps you to stretch a little further. Exhale as you go down. Come up slowly and inhale. Bend to the other side.
Repeat three times on each side.

17

Lesson 3

As you continue with the same exercise over a period of time you may notice that your performance and aptitude seems to vary from day to day. An exercise that you can do easily and well one day may seem unnecessarily difficult the next. You should not be discouraged, because this is quite natural and common.

There may be several explanations. It is possible that your concentration and your physical abilities are not as good on one day as on another because you are tired, worried or preoccupied. A wrong movement at the beginning or during an exercise, a minor distraction or even the wrong temperature in the room can affect your concentration and performance. Although it may be difficult at first, continue with your exercises. It will soon become apparent to you that the very qualities which yoga itself can provide will enable you to "turn off" and concentrate on your session in spite of any drawbacks.

Because when you do yoga you have to concentrate on several things at the same time your awareness and powers of observation will become greater. This, in turn, will help you to enhance the quality of your entire life. We are all inclined to function rather mechanically, without realizing why we act and react in the ways we do. As well as becoming more aware of other people, we should also become more aware of ourselves. We should try to discover why we are in a good or bad mood. It may well disclose something about ourselves which we would normally gloss over or ignore.

This awareness is a vital part of yoga, a system which is designed to benefit the mind as well as the body.

The exercises which follow are more advanced than those in the previous lessons. Do them slowly and do not strain. If you feel fatigued stop and do the relaxation pose. Continue only when you feel completely relaxed. It is a 30-minute programme and all these exercises are to be done, by both men and women, for one week. Begin as always by relaxing.

RELAXATION POSE

Lie on your back, feet slightly apart, arms at your sides, palms up and head and neck relaxed. Close your eyes. Put your tongue behind your lower teeth and relax your jaw. As always, breathe slowly and only through your nose. Try to relax your mind as well as your body. Remain like this for at least two minutes before and after each yoga session.

WARMING UP
Speeds up circulation, warms the whole body
If you or the room are cold you can do this before relaxation

1. Lie on your back. Relax head and neck, keeping them on the floor.
2. Clench fists and contract all your muscles, bending your feet up with the toes pointing towards your body. Inhale as you contract. Hold for a count of five.
Exhale and relax. Repeat twice.

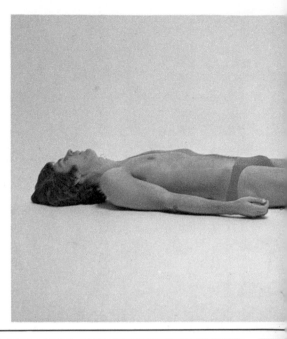

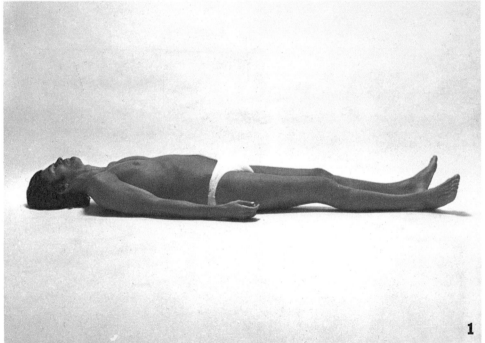

1

THE CROCODILE-2
Increases the suppleness of the spine, slims the waist
These movements must be done slowly, smoothly and without interruption and try not to stop at any point

1. Lie on your back with your arms outstretched and the right ankle crossed over the left. Inhale.
2. Twist your hips and legs to the right and turn your head as far as possible to the left.
3. Twist your hips and legs to the left and turn your head as far as possible to the right.
Repeat once, still holding your breath. Return to the starting position and exhale.
Repeat the whole exercise with the left ankle crossed over the right.

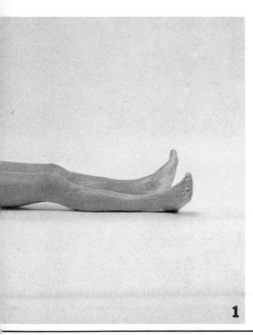 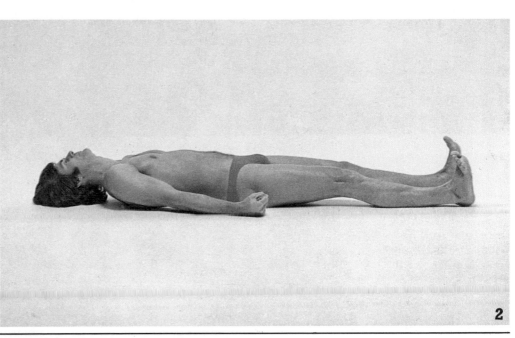

1   2

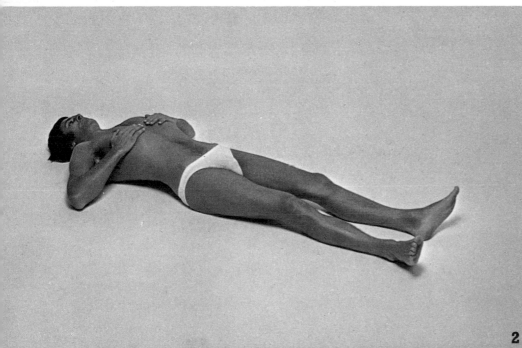

2

TOTAL BREATHING
Relaxes and calms, increases lung capacity

1. Begin inhaling abdominally.
2. Then inhale thoracically.
Then draw up the air so that your lungs are filled to capacity. Hold your breath for a moment, and start exhaling slowly.
When your lungs are completely empty pause, and then start inhaling again.
Repeat nine times.

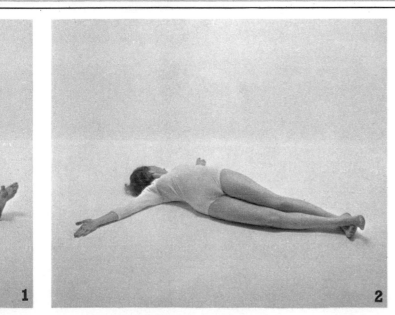 

1   2   3

KNEE–BENDING–3
Increases suppleness of the spine, stimulates the internal organs
This exercise should be done as slowly as possible

1. Lie on your back with both legs bent and hands clasped around your knees.
2 and 3. Rock backwards and forwards 10 times, trying to put the soles of your feet on the floor when you are upright. Tuck your chin into your chest so that your spine is rounded and one vertebra after the other comes into contact with the floor.

1

1

SQUATTING
Strengthens abdominal muscles, stretches the Achilles tendons and cures constipation

1. Squat with your soles flat on the floor and your knees and feet wide apart.
2. Stretch your arms forwards and link your hands in front.
3. Inhale and raise your arms as though you were holding an axe above your head. Look up.
Slowly bring your hands down to the floor and exhale, bending the head forwards.
Repeat three times.

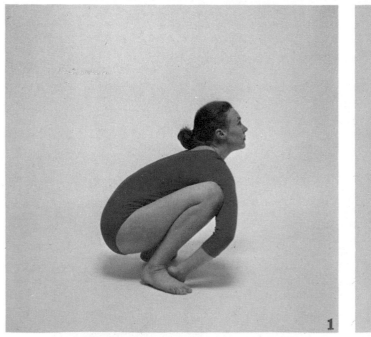

1

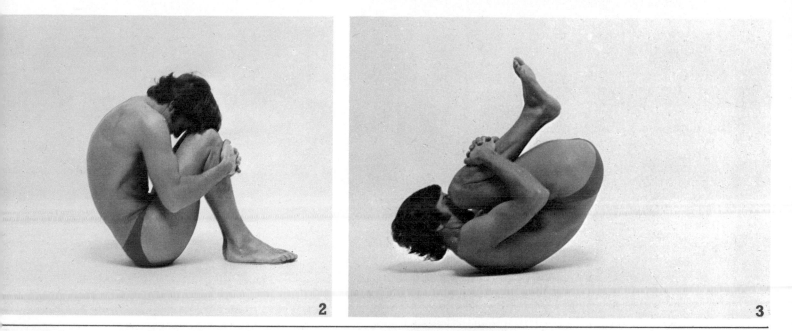

2

3

2

3

THE BACK STRETCH
Stretches and strengthens back muscles, pelvic region, inner thighs and legs

1. Bend your right leg and put the sole of the right foot on the inside of the left thigh, as high up as possible. The left leg should be slightly bent so that the knee is raised a few inches. Stretch your arms upwards.
2. Push your chin forward and twist your body to the left. Exhale and bend forward, keeping your back straight. Hold your left knee and breathe slowly to the mental count of 10. After the last exhalation raise your arms, inhale and stretch up, leaning slightly backwards. Repeat once.
3. Repeat twice with the left leg on the right thigh.

2

3

THE CAT
Counteracts hollow back, strengthens abdominal muscles

1. With hands and knees parallel and apart, bend your head down and look at your thighs. Do abdominal breathing six times, being careful to pull the abdomen in and up with each exhalation.
2. Inhale and arch your back inwards and raise your head. Repeat five times.

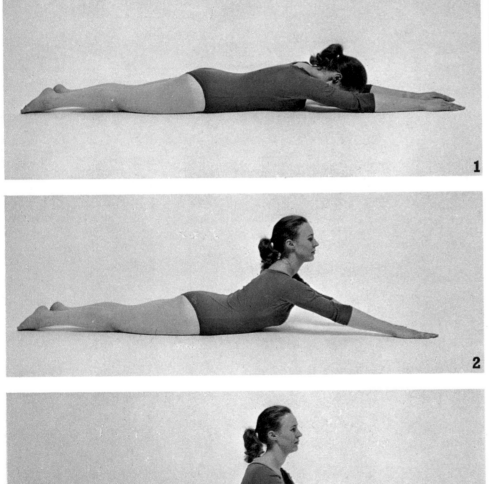

THE COBRA-3
Loosens and relaxes the back muscles, strengthens chin and neck muscles
This exercise differs from the Cobra in the first two lessons. When doing this Cobra your body should be completely relaxed

1. Lie face down, with your forehead on the floor and your arms stretched out in front of you, palms downwards.
2. With little steps, slowly raise your head and body using only your straight arms as support.
3. Come up as far as your navel. Breathing normally, remain in this posture for a mental count of 10. Slowly lower your body back to starting position. Repeat once.

THE TREE
Develops poise, good balance and strengthens leg muscles

Put the sole of your left foot against the inside of your right thigh, as high as possible. Raise your arms to shoulder height. Focus your eyes on a point straight ahead. Hold this posture for five breaths.

22

2

THE TRIANGLE-2
Slims waist and sides, strengthens spine
It is important in this exercise to bend sideways and not forward

With feet together, stand up straight and, with hands linked, stretch your arms above your head. Inhale.
Bend sideways, exhaling.
Inhale and straighten up.
Exhale and bend to the other side.
Repeat three times on each side.

Lesson 4

Most of us don't sit still very often, even for a few minutes. We are inclined to fidget and fiddle. You will find, however, that with the help of yoga you will be able to sit immobile for increasingly long periods of time.

Although there are some people for whom the Lotus posture—the classic yoga posture with crossed legs and feet high up on the thighs—is natural, for the majority it presents difficulties. But this posture is essential only for deep meditation, and, since deep meditation is not everybody's aim, it would be best for you to become proficient in easier sitting postures.

Every posture brings certain benefits. Some are calming, others help concentration and Vajrasana, the Thunderbolt, one of the few yoga poses which can be done immediately after a meal, aids digestion. It is advisable to discover which of the sitting postures are most comfortable for you. Then learn to relax in it. Your back and head must always be in a straight line and if, when you begin, you find that you cannot sit straight without discomfort, lean against the wall or a piece of furniture until you find that you can manage without it.

Use a sitting posture to relax between sitting exercises. The best way to make the most of these short rests is by closing your eyes and trying to relax your mind with the help of slow, deep breathing.

The following exercises, which are to be done for one week, are for both men and women. Each session will take you about 30 minutes. Begin by relaxing.

RELAXATION POSE

Lie on your back, feet slightly apart, arms at your side, palms up and head and neck relaxed. Feel that all the little muscles in your cheeks relax. Imagine that a hand is slowly stroking your hair and relax scalp. As always, breathe only through your nose. Try to relax your mind as well as your body. Remain like this for at least two minutes before and after each yoga session.

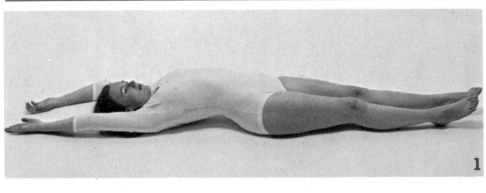

1

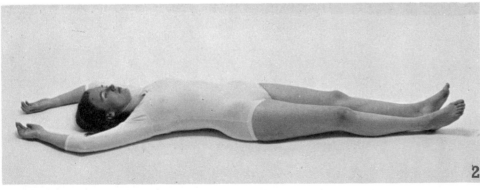

2

THE STICK POSE

Stretches and slims sides and waist, tones back, arm and leg muscles

1. Lie on your back with your arms stretched over your head. Inhale and stretch your whole body, including your arms and legs. Hold for a mental count of five.
2. Exhale, release stretch and contract all the muscles on either side of the spine, pressing the small of your back against the floor. Hold for the count of five.
Repeat three times.

THE CROCODILE-3

Increases the suppleness of the spine, slims the waist
The movements must be done slowly and without interruption

1. Lie on your back with your arms outstretched at shoulder height. Rest the heel of your right foot on the toes of your left foot.

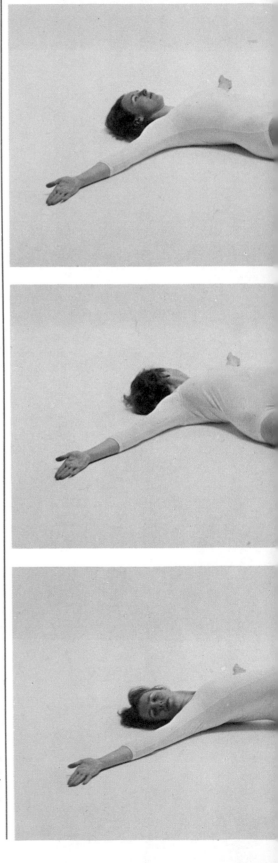

2. Inhale. Twist your hips and legs to the right and turn your head as far as possible to the left.
3. Twist your hips and legs to the left and turn your head as far as possible to the right.
Repeat once, still holding your breath. Exhale and relax.
Repeat the whole exercise with the left foot resting on the right.

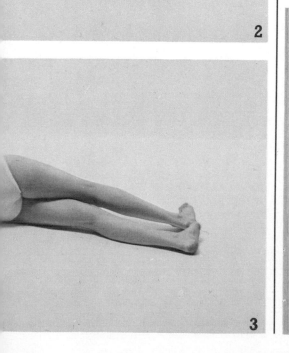

1

2

3

TOTAL BREATHING
Relaxes and calms, increases lung capacity

1. Begin inhaling abdominally.
2. Then breathe thoracically.
Then draw up the air so that your lungs are filled to capacity. Hold your breath for a count of five. Then exhale slowly.
When your lungs are completely empty pause, and then begin inhaling again.

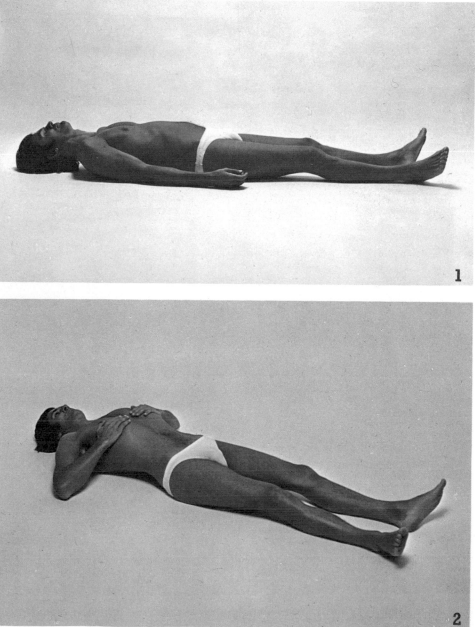

1

2

THE PRAYING MANTIS
Makes the knees stronger and more supple

1. Squat with your feet apart and the soles on the floor. Put your hands together in a praying position. Bend your elbows so they touch the insides of your knees. Inhale. Press your knees outwards with your elbows and raise your head.
2. Exhale, press your knees in, stretch your arms and hands to the floor, and bend your head forwards. Repeat four times.

1

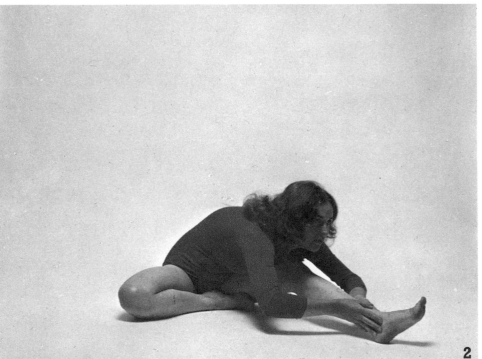

2

2

THE BACK STRETCH-2
Stretches and strengthens back and slims inner thighs and waist

1. Bend your right leg and put the sole of your right foot against the inside of your left thigh, as high as possible. Stretch your arms up.
2. Push your chin forward and twist your body to the left. Exhale and bend forward, keeping your back straight. Breathing calmly, hold the leg as far down as you can for a mental count of 10.
After the last exhalation raise your arms, inhale and stretch up, leaning slightly backwards.
Repeat with your left leg bent

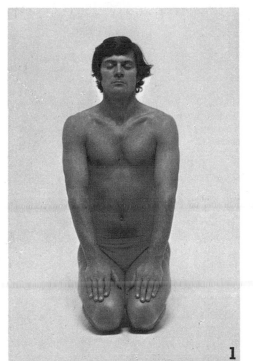

THE THUNDERBOLT
Makes knees and ankles more supple, aids digestion
This posture, which forms the basis of various other asanas, is one of the few which can be done immediately after eating

1. Kneel with your big toes together and your heels apart. Sit back on your feet, keeping your head and back in a straight line. Relax your shoulders and place your hands palms down on the top of your knees.
2. This posture can also be done with your palms upwards, on top of each other, at the top of your thighs.

SPINE-TWISTING
Keeps the spine supple, loosens tension at the back of the neck and in the spine

1. Starting in the Thunderbolt position, keep your right hand on your right thigh and stretch your left leg out behind you. Bend your left arm and put your forearm behind your back so that your hand holds the inside of your right elbow.
2. Turn your head slowly to the left, as far as possible.
3. Turn your head slowly round to the right, as far as possible.
4. Repeat with right leg behind you and right forearm behind your back.

27

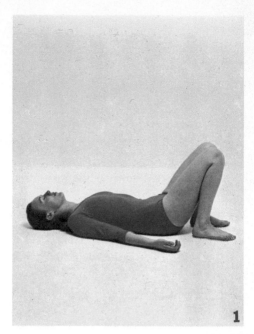

1

2

THE STEADY SEAT
A sitting posture in which most people feel relaxed and comfortable

Kneel with your knees wide apart. Bring your right foot forward and put the sole against the inside of your left thigh, as high as possible. Make sure that both buttocks are resting on the floor with your weight evenly distributed. Relax with your hands resting on your knees, palms upwards.

Repeat, putting the sole of your left foot against the inside of your right thigh.

THE SHOULDER BOW
Strengthens and increases the suppleness of the spine

1. Lie on your back. Put your feet about 15 inches apart, drawn back towards your body, with the soles on the floor. Put your arms at your sides, with the palms of your hands facing upwards.
2. Inhale and arch your back, your weight resting on your shoulders.
3. Exhale and slowly lower your back, beginning at the top and putting down one vertebra after the other.

Repeat three times.

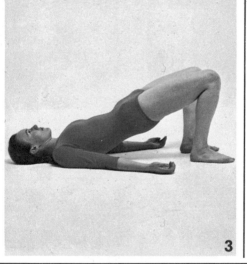

3

THE LOCUST PREPARATION

Lie on your abdomen with your arms at your sides and your chin resting on the floor. Raise your buttocks, and "walk" as far forward as you can on your toes, resting your weight on your shoulders. Stay for a count of 10. Walk slowly back and relax.

THE TREE
Develops poise and good balance, strengthens leg muscles

Put the sole of your left foot against the inside of your right thigh, as high up as possible. Raise your arms to shoulder height. Focus your eyes on a point straight ahead. Hold for as long as you can. Repeat with your right foot against your left thigh.

THE PALM TREE
Develops poise and good balance, slims waist and sides

Stand with your feet parallel and together. Put your hands together and stretch up. Rise up on your toes and, raising your head, look up at your hands. Hold for five breaths. Do this exercise once a day for three days. On the fourth day begin the variation.

Stretch one leg back and bend your body forward. Keep your arms outstretched in front of you and look at your hands. Raise your head slowly and bring your leg down. Repeat with the other leg.

Lesson 5

One of the particular benefits of yoga is that you can learn appreciation of silence and solitude instead of being frightened by it.

Many people deliberately surround themselves with a blanket of perpetual noise and activity. But continuous noise can have a blunting effect on the nervous system. Naturally, you will try to practise your yoga in a quiet place and in silence. Try to prolong this silence afterwards and do not, for example, immediately switch on the radio or television.

The following exercise, The Creation of Warmth, which takes about 10 minutes, should not be included in your daily 30-minute practice session, but it can be done at any time. Do not practise in a cold room and, if you feel cold, cover yourself with a blanket. The warmth you are creating will be a pleasant and relaxing influence on all the internal organs. There is nothing magical in this. It is the result of your concentration and relaxation.

Lie flat on your back with your feet apart and your knees bent and together. Put your hands on your stomach so that your fingertips almost meet. Close your eyes and breathe from the stomach to the small of the back and then the other way. Concentrate on your slow and rhythmic breath, trying to exclude all other thoughts. You will gradually feel a sensation of warmth relaxing this whole area. If you find it difficult to get to sleep, practise this exercise at night in bed. And, if you can spare the time, also practise it in the morning.

The following exercises, which are for both men and women are to be done every day for a week, or of course longer if it is necessary. Each session will take you about 30 minutes. Begin with relaxation and total breathing.

THE RELAXATION POSE
Lie on your back, feet slightly apart, arms at your sides, palms up and head and neck relaxed. Feel that all the little muscles in your cheeks relax. Imagine that a hand is slowly stroking your hair and relax your scalp. As always, breathe only through your nose. Try to relax your mind as well as your body. Do this for at least two minutes before and after each session.

TOTAL BREATHING
Begin inhaling abdominally and then breathe thoracically. Then draw up the air so that your lungs are filled to capacity. Hold your breath for a count of five. Then exhale slowly. When your lungs are empty pause, then begin inhaling again. Repeat six times.

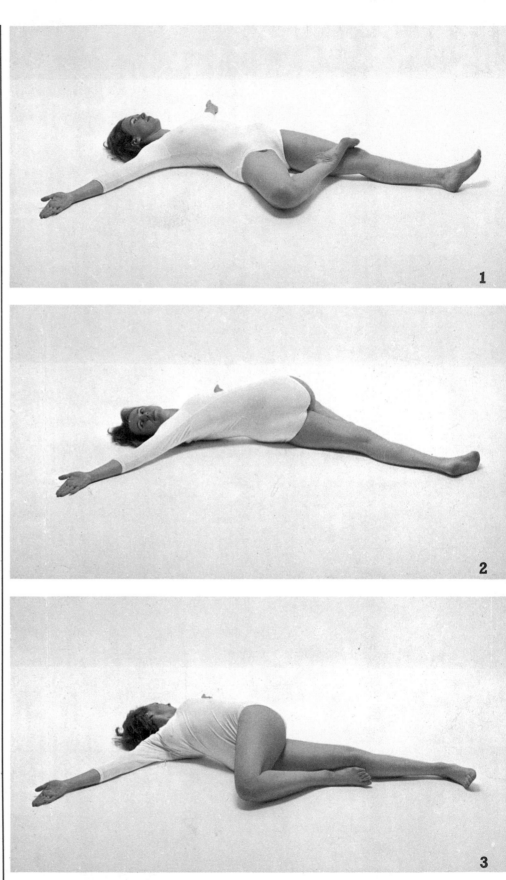

1

2

3

THE CROCODILE—4
Increases the suppleness of the spine and slims the waist

1. Lie on your back with your arms outstretched at shoulder height. Put your right ankle on your left leg, just above the knee. Inhale.
2. Twist your hips and legs to the left and turn your head as far as possible to the right.
Twist your hips and legs to the right and turn your head as far as possible to the left.
Repeat, still holding your breath. Return to the beginning. Exhale.
3. Repeat with your left ankle on your right leg.

1

2

3

1

2

3

SPINAL MASSAGE
Increases the suppleness of the spine and improves balance

1. Hook your left foot under your right knee and clasp your hands around your left knee. Keep your right leg straight.
2. Swing slowly up and down 10 times, coming to a sitting position each time.
3. Try to make your right leg parallel to the floor at the top of the swing. The important thing, however, is to keep your leg straight. Repeat 10 times with your right foot under your left knee and your hands around your right knee.

THE SHOULDER BOW
Strengthens and increases the suppleness of the spine

1. Lie on your back with your feet about 15 inches apart, soles on the floor, and as close to your body as possible. Put your arms at your sides, with your palms facing up.
2. Inhale and arch your back, resting your weight on your shoulders and feet.
3. Exhale and slowly lower your back, beginning at the top and putting down one vertebra after the other.
Repeat three times.

THE SIDE-STRETCH RELAXATION
Relaxes, induces sleep

Lie on your left side with your left arm outstretched under your head. Put your right arm behind your back with your hand touching the floor. Bend your right leg so that your knee rests on the floor. Your left leg can be either slightly bent or straight.

Close your eyes. Hold for at least one minute, then repeat on your right side.

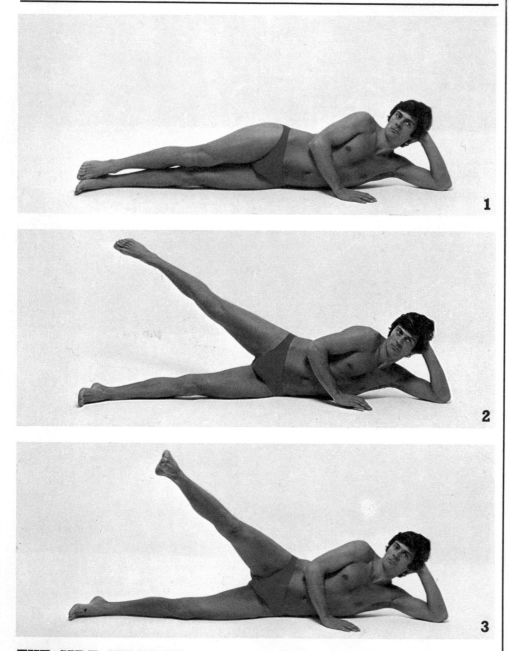

THE SIDE STRETCH
Strengthens the muscles in the midriff, waist and legs

1. Support your head with your left hand and put your right hand on the floor in front of you. Your legs should be straight and together. The whole body, from your elbow to your toes, should be straight.

2. Raise your right leg as high as you can, keeping it straight.
3. Lower your leg a few inches. Pointing your toes, draw a line through the air with your foot, first forwards and then backwards, three times.
Lower your leg to the floor and relax.
Repeat on your right side.

THE THUNDERBOLT-2
Strengthens back, slims waist

1. Sit in the Thunderbolt posture.
2. Raise your body, keeping your back straight, and sit on the right side of your legs.
Raise your body and sit on the left. Repeat five times on each side.
Raise your arms above your head.
3. Keeping your back straight, raise your body and sit on the left side of your legs, moving your arms to the right. Straighten, and, keeping your arms up, sit on the right of your legs. Move your arms to the left. Repeat three times on each side.

1

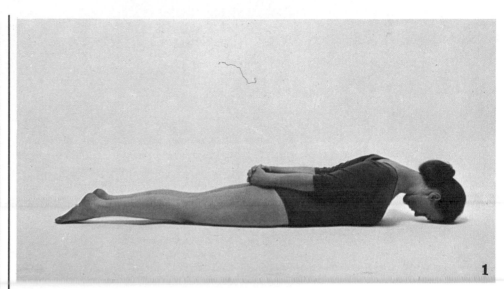

1

2

2

3

THE CROW WALK
Strengthens and firms thighs, calves, knees and Achilles tendons
This exercise is also good preparation for the Half Lotus and Lotus. Ideally it should be done with the soles of your feet on the floor, but if you cannot do this, you can do it with raised heels

Squat with your hands on your knees. Walk around the room, keeping your legs as close together as possible. Count your steps and try to increase the number each day. But, as with all yoga exercises, do not strain.

THE COBRA-4
Strengthens back muscles, stimulates the abdominal organs, increases flexibility of the shoulders

1. Lie on your abdomen with your forehead on the floor. Stretch your arms behind your back and clasp your hands together.
2. Inhale. Raise your head, shoulders, chest and arms as much as possible. Mentally count to six, holding your breath and keeping your arms straight. Exhale.
3. Repeat, with your hands holding your elbows behind your back.

1

1

THE HALF LOCUST
Increases control of the body by using muscles on one side while the other side is relaxed
This exercise is done as a complementary pose after The Cobra

1. Lie on your abdomen with your chin on the floor. Keep your feet together and put your arms at your sides. Contract your muscles in the small of the right side of your back and lean on your right arm. Raise your right leg without taking the hip from the floor, keeping the leg straight. It is not important how high your leg goes as long as you remember to relax the side of your body which is not contracted.
2. Repeat, raising your left leg.

2

2

1

2

3

3

THE BACK STRETCH–3
Stretches and strengthens back, slims inner thighs and waist

1. Sit on the floor with your left leg straight and right leg bent. Inhale. Stretch your arms above your head and lean slightly backwards.
2. Exhale and bend forwards, putting your hands on your left knee. Breathing calmly, move your hands as far down your leg as you can, and hold for a mental count of 10. After the last exhalation raise your arms, inhale and stretch up. Repeat once.
3. Repeat with your left leg bent and your right leg straight.

THE WALKING CAT
Increases the suppleness of the spine

1. Kneel on your hands and knees, keeping your back straight.
2. Without moving your legs, make little steps to the left with your hands until your left hand is parallel with your left knee.
3. Move back to the centre and continue around to the right until your right hand is parallel with your right knee.
Repeat three times.

1 **2**

THE RUDDER
Loosens neck muscles and the whole shoulder area, slims waist

Stand with your feet wide apart, with your hands linked behind your back. Bend forward from your waist, keeping your back straight. Look up and raise your arms as high as possible. With your chin pointing forward, turn slowly to the right and then to the left. Repeat four times, moving slowly and rhythmically from one side to the other. Return to the centre, straighten and relax.

1

2

3

THE TRIANGLE- 3
Improves balance and co-ordination, tones the abdominal region, slims the waist

1. Stand with your feet well apart. Stretch your arms above your head, putting the palms of your hands together. Look up at your hands.
2. Turn your body and your right foot to the right. Continue looking up.
3. Bend your right knee and transfer your weight to your right leg. Lower your body as far as possible, keeping an upright position. Return to the starting position, still looking up.
Repeat, turning to the left.
Repeat twice.

Lesson 6

Although yoga has a number of the physical elements of gymnastics—balance, poise, posture, concentration—the two exercise disciplines have fundamental differences. In gymnastics (and in other forms of physical exercise) concentration is directed outward. In yoga, there is total inner concentration and observation of the functioning of the body.

This is often a major problem when people begin yoga. We are all accustomed to having our attention easily distracted, and the withdrawal of the senses, so necessary to reap the full rewards of yoga, is a completely new experience to understand and master.

To help in overcoming this obstacle, you should become more aware of the ways you are using your eyes, closing and relaxing them in some exercises and focusing them to help you balance in others, such as The Tree.

Another basic difference between yoga and most other forms of exercise is its lack of competitive spirit. This, too, might be difficult to accept for someone who has been accustomed to the challenge of competition and the satisfaction of winning. In yoga, you are not out to beat anyone. It does not matter if your performance is far from perfect. What is important it that you try to do your best.

Yoga postures should not be demonstrated as a party piece. Your yoga should be something special and personal which helps you—and then helps others through your development.

This lesson, like the five previous ones, is designed for both men and women and should take about 30 minutes. As usual, start by relaxing.

THE RELAXATION POSE

Lie on your back, feet slightly apart, arms at your sides, palms up and head and neck relaxed. Feel that all the little muscles in your cheeks relax. Imagine that a hand is slowly stroking your hair and relaxing your scalp. Breathe only through your nose. Try to relax your mind as well as your body. Remain like this for two minutes before and after each yoga session.

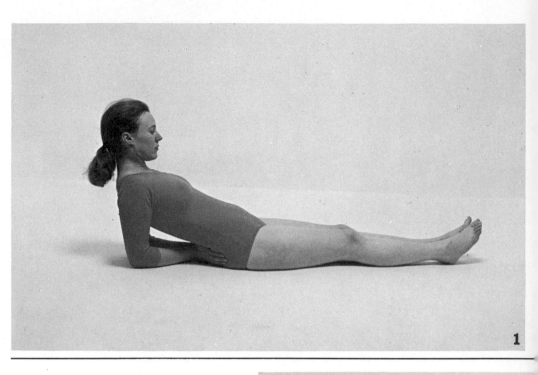

1

THE CROCODILE—5
Counteracts hollow back, increases the suppleness of the spine, slims the waist

1. Lie on your back with your arms outstretched at shoulder height. Bend your knees, bringing your feet up as close to your body as possible. Inhale.
2. Keeping your legs, knees and feet together, twist your hips and legs to the right and turn your head as far as possible to the left.
3. Twist your hips and legs to the left and turn your head as far as possible to the right.
Repeat once, still holding your breath.
Return to the starting position, stretch your legs and exhale.

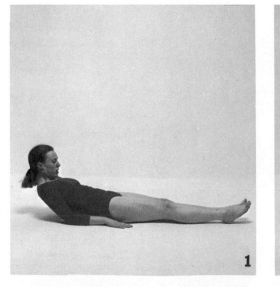

1

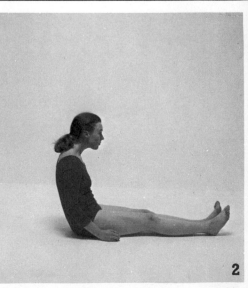

2

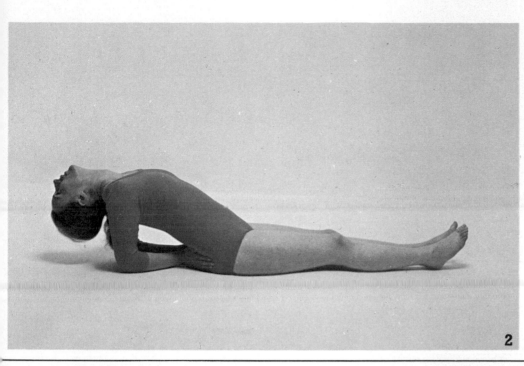

THORACIC BREATHING—2
Increases the flexibility of the ribcage and the expansion of the lungs

Lie on your back with your hands on your ribcage and your fingertips touching. Slightly tense your abdomen. Inhale, filling your chest with air and forcing your fingertips apart. Try not to expand the abdomen as you inhale. Exhale and feel your ribs move inwards and your fingertips join.
1. Support yourself on your elbows. Bring your wrists together behind your back with the palms of your hands against your body.
2. Arch your back and drop your head backwards. In this position concentrate on expanding and contracting your ribcage.
Take 10 slow breaths.

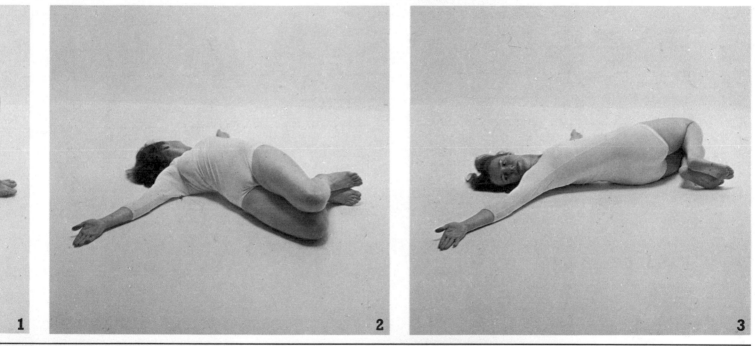

CURLING UP
Strengthens the lower back and abdominal muscles, couteracts hollow back

Lie on your back with the palms of your hands downwards. Relax.
1,2. Inhaling slowly, raise your head, shoulders and back until you are sitting upright. If you have difficulty help yourself with your elbows.
3. Bend your head back as you finish inhaling.
4. Tuck your chin in and begin exhaling slowly. With your back rounded, lower your body to the floor so that your vertabrae seem to touch the floor one after the other. Repeat twice.

LEG EXERCISE
Tones up all the leg muscles, increases the suppleness of the knees

Sit upright with your legs straight.
1. Keeping your left leg straight, clasp your right leg with both hands at the back of the thigh and raise it towards your chest.
2. Without moving your thigh, draw a circle in the air with your right leg from the knee downwards. Circle five times in one direction, then five times in the other direction. Repeat with your left leg raised.

1

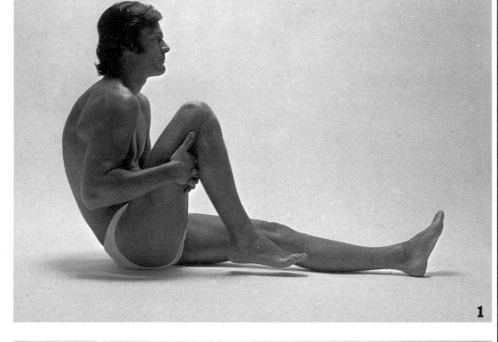

1

3

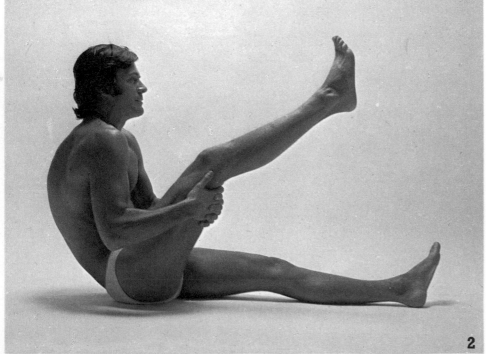

2

5

2

SHOULDER-STAND PREPARATION
Stimulates circulation in the legs, eases varicose veins

Before beginning this exercise, lie on the floor and put your hand underneath your back. If there is a hollow between your back and the floor, put a small, soft, rolled-up towel in the hollow.
1. Bend your knees and, keeping your hands on the floor, slowly raise your feet until your legs are almost vertical.
2. Breathe normally in this position and, with your legs relaxed, flex your ankles in all directions. Bend your knees again and bring your legs down to the floor.
Repeat twice.

1

4

THE BALANCE
Strengthens thighs and legs, stretches hamstrings, improves co-ordination and concentration

1. Sit with your knees bent and hold your big toes.
2. Breathing slowly and evenly, raise your legs and lean slightly backwards, keeping your knees and heels together.
3,4,5. When you are balancing on your buttocks, straighten your legs as much as possible, still holding your toes. Hold for a count of five. Slowly bend your knees again, still holding your toes, and return to the starting position.

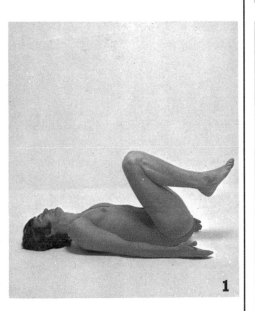

1

2

2

THE RABBIT
Increases suppleness of the spine and shoulders, strengthens arms and slims

Sitting on your heels in the Thunderbolt posture, link your hands behind your back.
1. Keeping your eyes closed, push your chin forward and exhale. With your back as straight as possible, bend forward and put your forehead on the floor.
2. Inhale and stretch your arms up as much as possible.
Exhale and lower your arms.
Repeat twice.

1

2

POSE OF THE CHILD
Relaxes and calms, induces sleep

1. From the Rabbit posture stretch your arms out in front of you with elbows bent. Breathe slowly and rhythmically. Hold this pose as long as possible.

2. This pose can also be done with your arms at the sides of your body with the palms of your hands facing upwards.

THE PARCEL
Slims the hips and stomach, increases the suppleness of the knees, strengthens the shoulders

1. Lie face down. Bend your knees and hold your ankles.

2. Breathing normally, swing your body to the right until you are lying on your right side.
Swing over to the left until you are lying on your left side.
Repeat five times.

1

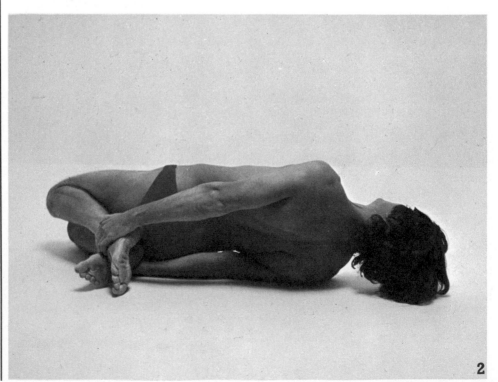

2

1

2

THE COBRA—5
Strengthens chin, neck and back muscles

Lie face down with your fingertips level to your shoulders and your forehead on the floor. Slowly push your chin forward. Inhale and raise your head, shoulders and chest.
1. Raise your head a little higher and, holding your breath, slowly turn your head to the left as far as possible.
2. Slowly turn your head to the right as far as possible.
Exhale as you lower your head.
Repeat twice.

THE TRIANGLE—4
Stretches and tones the whole body, stimulates circulation

Stand with your legs well apart. Inhale and stretch your arms so that your arms and legs form an X shape. Exhale. Bend down and try to rest your hands on your feet, or clasp the back of your ankles. Inhale and stretch up. Repeat twice.

Lesson 7

Although yoga has become extremely popular in the West, many people are not quite clear about what it is and what it stands for. Yoga is certainly not a religion, although some of its paths aim at union with the highest principle. Yoga is not, despite attempts to make it so, a cult. Yoga is not merely physical exercises—although one path, *hatha* yoga, includes these. Yoga is not a means of retiring from the world and becoming a hermit or a celibate, although here again there is one path for those who want to lead a single-minded, spiritual life.

Yoga is, first and foremost, a scientific system of physical and mental health. It has proved its value over thousands of years and the findings of scientific research which has been done on it are testament to the remarkable insight and intelligence of the men who evolved this system.

There are many paths of yoga, paths to the union of the individual's spirit with the universal spirit, the transcendental consciousness. The four best known are *hatha*, *karma*, *bhakti* and *gyana*. *Karma* means action, and *karma* yoga is practised by people on behalf of others. It is the yoga of good works and kindness.

Bhakti yoga is deeply devotional and strives for union with God through prayer and love.

Gyana yoga follows the mental rational path, working towards the goal through developing the intellect.

These then, are the four main strands of yoga:
Hatha—the yoga of mastery over the mind and body
Karma—the yoga of good works
Bhakti—the yoga of faith and devotion
Gyana—the yoga of study and knowledge

In addition, there are other paths including *raja* yoga, the yoga of rigid mental control, and *manta* yoga, the yoga of the mystical meanings of sounds.

This course is concerned with *hatha* yoga, the path through mastering the body and mind which most people in the West think of when they consider yoga.

This lesson, like the ones before, is designed for men and women and should take about 30 minutes. As usual, start by relaxing.

THE RELAXATION POSE
Lie on your back, feet slightly apart, arms at your sides, palms up and head and neck relaxed. Close your lower teeth and relax your jaw. As always, breathe only through your nose. Try to relax your mind as well as your body. Remain like this for at least two minutes before and after each yoga session.

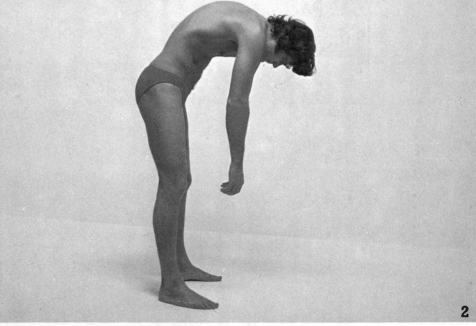

THE STANDING BREATH
Improves breath control, stimulates circulation of the blood

Stand with your feet about 14 inches apart, your arms hanging loosely at your sides and your whole body completely relaxed. Close your eyes. Inhale deeply, from the abdomen into the thorax and upper part of the lungs.
1. Exhale slowly, bending forward and letting your relaxed body hang down from your waist. Remain in this posture for a few seconds without inhaling.
2. Inhaling, slowly raise your body, pulling yourself up with the muscles in your back and shoulders. Coordinate the inhalation with the movement so that it is completed when you are standing up straight. Repeat twice.

NECK EXERCISE
Relaxes neck and shoulders, relieves headaches

1. Kneel and sit on your heels. Inhale. Bend your arms and point your elbows upwards behind your back, and bend your head as far back as possible.
2. Keeping your elbows bent at the same angle, swing your arms forward and bend your head forward with your chin touching your chest. Repeat twice.
Relax your arms and exhale.

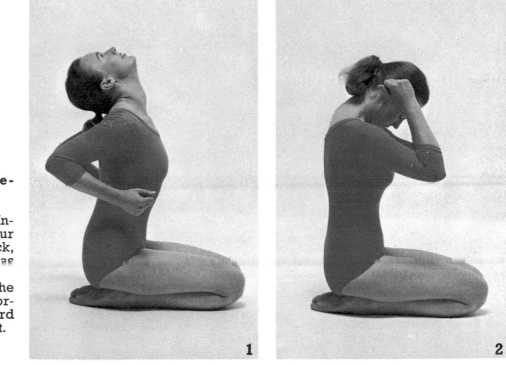

HAMSTRING EXERCISE
Strengthens legs, ankles and feet, stretches and lengthens hamstrings.

1. Stand on your feet and hands, keeping your legs straight and your head down. Look at your knees.
2. Without moving your hands or your head, raise your heels so that you are standing on your toes. Repeat five times, slowly and rhythmically.
3. Bend your left knee and stand on the toes of your left foot, pressing down firmly on your right heel.
4. Keeping your left foot flat on the floor and your left leg straight, bend your right knee and stand on the toes of your right foot. Press down firmly on your left heel.
Repeat five times, slowly and rhythmically and without moving your hands or head.

 **1**

 **2**

THE THUNDERBOLT–3
Slims sides and waist, relieves tension in the shoulders

1. Sit on your heels, in the Thunderbolt posture. Clasp your hands behind your head, keeping your elbows back as far as possible.
2. Inhale. Bend to the right from your waist. Exhale. Tighten your abdomen muscles slightly. Inhale as you straighten up.
3. Bend to the left and exhale. Inhale as you straighten up.
Repeat three times.

THE PLOUGH
Increases the flexibility of the spinal column, stimulates the nervous system, massages the internal organs

1. Lie on your back. Raise your legs, with your upper arms and elbows on the floor and your hands supporting your back. Keep your chin tucked in. Having placed a stack of books at the right distance from your head, swing your legs backwards, pushing up with your elbows to support your hips.
2. Keeping your legs straight, try to put your toes on top of the books. Put your arms on the floor with the palms of your hands down. Hold for a count of 10. Support your back and roll down slowly. Do not raise your head.
3. As you continue to practice this exercise, slowly reduce the height of the support until you are able to touch the ground.

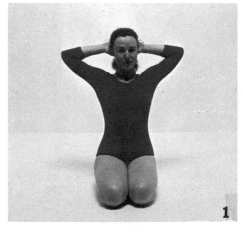 **1**

 **2**

 **3**

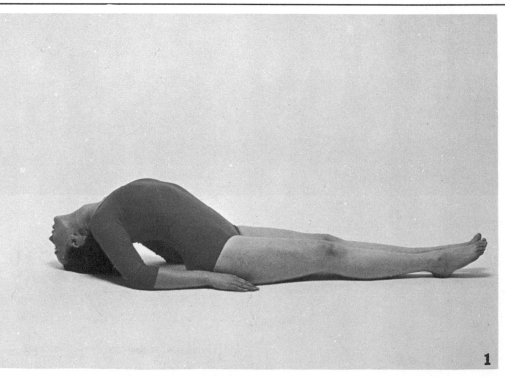 **1**

THE BACK STRETCH–4
Strengthens the pelvic region, stretches back muscles and hamstrings, slims waist

1. Sit with your legs as wide apart as possible. Stretch your arms above your head.
2. Twist from your waist towards the left. Bend forward to your left leg, keeping your back straight and your arms stretched out on your legs.

Point your chin forward and look up. Hold for a mental count of five. Inhale and sit up again with your arms still stretched. Turn to the front.
3. Twist from your waist to the right. Bend forward to your right leg, keeping your back straight, your chin up, and your arms stretched out on your leg. Hold for a count of five. Inhale and sit up.
Repeat twice on each side.

3

1

2

3

2

THE FISH
Flexes the spine, stretches the neck muscles and abdomen
This is one of the counterposes for the Plough and should always be done after it

Lie on your back with your legs together and your arms parallel to your body.
1. Raise yourself on your elbows. Arch your back as much as possible and drop your head back until it rests on the crown, sliding your elbows forward as you do this.
2. If you can, stretch your arms and put your hands on your thighs. Take three deep breaths. Put your elbows back on the floor. Slowly raise your head and lie flat.

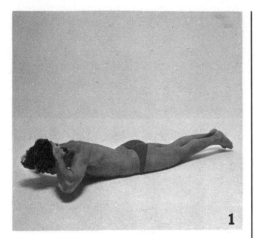

1

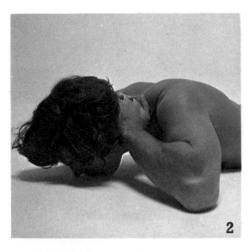

2

3

THE FIGHT
Strengthens and relaxes muscles in the neck and shoulders

Lie face down. Link your hands behind your neck, with your elbows on the floor.
1, 2. Inhale. Try to hold your head down but contract the muscles at both sides of the back of your neck and shoulders so that you slowly force your head and elbows to rise.
3. When you have raised your head as much as possible, hold for a count of 10. Now reverse the posture. Your head and shoulders "want" to stay up while your hands and arms are pressing down. Gradually reach the starting position. Do not repeat.

THE INVERTED BOAT
Strengthens the muscles in the legs, abdomen and lower back

1. Lie face down with your arms stretched out on the floor in front of you and your chin on the floor.
2. Inhale and raise your head, arms and legs. Hold for a count of five. Gradually try to increase the time you can hold this pose.

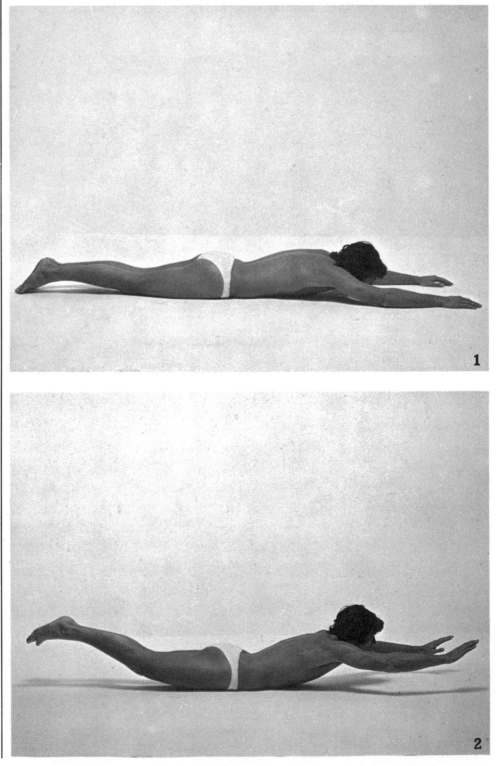

1

2

1

2

3

THE TREE
Develops poise and balance, strengthens leg muscles

1. Stand with your feet well apart and your arms at shoulder height.
2. Put the sole of your left foot against the inside of your right thigh, as high as possible. Focus your eyes on a point straight ahead. Hold this posture for five breaths and, if you feel quite steady, try closing your eyes and holding for another five breaths.
3. Repeat with the sole of your right foot against your left thigh.

Lesson 8

It might seem strange, if not pretentious, to consider yoga in connection with all the things that happen to you in your everyday life. This may seem particularly odd, since you have been told to look on your yoga sessions as half an hour totally divorced from the rest of your daily life.

Yet everyone who takes up yoga seriously—and that should include you—will in time notice certain changes beyond the expected physical improvements in posture, fitness and suppleness. These changes vary from person to person and, sometimes, are almost imperceptible.

Consider yourself since you began this yoga course. Can you detect any change in your mental attitude? Things which upset or worried you before may now seem less important or easier to cope with. This does not mean you have reached a state of detachment from worldly things, but it does indicate that you have shed some of the unnecessary psychological ballast you have been carrying.

This attitude is not cold, impersonal and indifferent. Rather, it can enable you to have a more objective approach to life and to evaluate situations and relationships more rationally. Yoga, with its relaxation and inward concentration, can and should produce this invaluable state of mind.

Some of the postures in this lesson are repeated from previous ones or are variations of previous exercises. This is necessary for several reasons. First, it takes time to really master some of these postures. In other cases it is vital that one particular pose be followed by another. In many instances, too, you can only build up to a position, such as the Shoulder-stand, gradually. It requires patience and practice. Yoga cannot be mastered overnight.

This lesson, like previous ones, is designed for both men and women and should take about 30 minutes. As always, begin by relaxing.

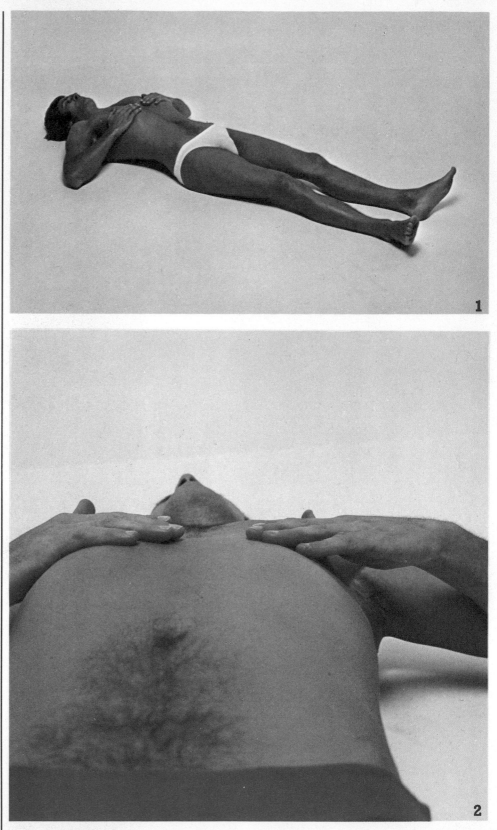

THE RELAXATION POSE
Lie on your back with your feet slightly apart, your arms at your sides, your palms up and your head and neck relaxed. Close your eyes. Put your tongue behind your teeth and relax your jaw. As always, breathe only through your nose. Try to relax your mind as well as your body. Remain like this for at least two minutes before and after each yoga session.

THORACIC BREATHING—3
Increases the flexibility of the ribcage, strengthens the chest muscles

1. Lie on your back. Slightly tense your abdomen. Put your hands on both sides of your ribcage. Inhale. Fill your chest with air and feel your ribs move sideways and outwards. Exhale and feel your ribs move inwards and your fingertips touch. Repeat six times.
2. With the next inhalation expand only the left side of your ribcage, keeping the right side relaxed. Exhale.
With the next inhalation expand only the right side of your ribcage, keeping the left side relaxed. Exhale.
Repeat six times.

1

2

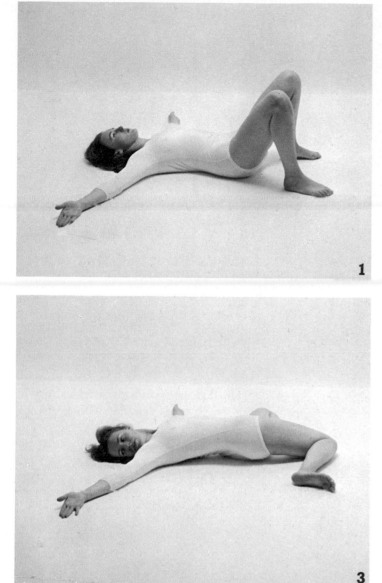

3

THE CROCODILE—6
Strengthens the lower back, slims the waist

1. Lie on your back with your arms outstretched at shoulder level. Bend your knees and keep your feet flat on the floor about 30 inches apart. Inhale.
2. Twist your hips and legs to the right, trying to bring your right knee to the floor and your left knee on to the sole of your right foot, and turn your head to the left.
3. Twist your hips and legs to the left, bringing your left knee to the floor and your right knee down to the sole of your left foot, and turn your head to the right.
Repeat once, still holding your breath.

THE BOAT
Strengthens abdominal and back muscles

Lie on your back. Inhale. Raise your head, shoulders and legs, keeping your arms and legs straight. Your head and feet should be on the same level and not more than six inches from the floor. Hold for a count of 10.
Exhale and relax.
Repeat once.

THE BOUND SEAT
A relaxing pose for people who find it difficult to sit in a cross-legged position
The belt will help you to keep your back erect

Sit with your legs straight. Then cross your legs and bring your knees up to your chest, keeping your back straight. Using a soft sash or belt, tie yourself, or ask someone to tie you up, in this position. Sit with your eyes closed for several minutes, relaxing your mind.

THE BACK STRETCH–5
Stretches back muscles and hamstrings, slims waist

1. Sit with your legs as wide apart as possible. Stretch your arms above your head. Exhale.
2. Twist from your waist towards the left. Bend forward to your left leg, keeping your back straight and your arms stretched out in front of you. Point your chin forward and look up. Hold for a count of five. Inhale and sit up, with your arms still stretched. Turn to the front.
3. Exhale and repeat to your right.
4. Only do this variation if you feel you are sufficiently supple. Exhale and bend forward, keeping your back straight. Hold your ankles or toes and try to touch the floor with your chin. Relax in this position and hold for a count of five. Inhale and straighten up.

THE PLOUGH
Increases the flexibility of the spine, stimulates the nervous system, massages the internal organs

Lie on your back. Raise your legs, with your elbows on the floor and your hands supporting your back. Keep your chin tucked in. Swing your legs backwards, pushing up with your arms to support your hips.
1. With your legs straight, put your toes on top of a pile of books or a low stool. Put your arms on the floor with the palms of your hands down. Hold for a count of 10. Support your back and roll down slowly, keeping your knees close to your chest. Do not raise your head.
2. As you continue to practise this posture, you should be able to reach the floor with your toes. Keep your legs straight.

THE HALF SHOULDER-STAND
Increases the circulation, improves the complexion

Lie on your back with your arms at your sides. Bend your knees and slowly raise your legs to a vertical position. Swing your legs back towards your head, using your hands to support your back as it leaves the floor. Rise up, supporting your hips with your hands. Keep your chin tucked in. Remain in this position for as long as you feel comfortable, breathing deeply. Then bring your knees as close to your head as possible and uncurl your spine, keeping your legs close to your body. Keeping your head on the floor, return to the starting position.

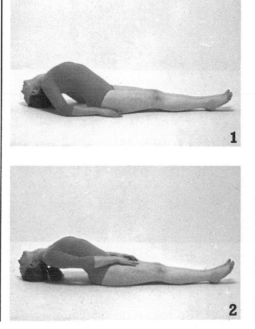

THE FISH
Flexes the spine, stretches the neck muscles and abdomen
This is one of the counterposes for the Plough and Shoulderstand and should be done after those postures

Lie on your back with your legs together and your arms at your sides.
1. Supporting yourself with your elbows, raise your upper body. Arch your back and drop your head back until it rests on the crown, sliding your elbows forward as you do this.
2. If you can, stretch your arms forward and put your hands on your thighs. Take three deep breaths. Put your elbows back on the floor. Slowly raise your head and then lie flat.

THE SIMPLE TWIST
Tones up the nervous system, relieves backache, slims waist

1. Sit on the floor with your legs straight. Bend your right knee and put your right foot outside your left knee. Turning from your waist, twist your upper body and head as far as possible to the right. Place the palms of your hands on the floor. Keep your buttocks firmly on the floor and try to keep your back relaxed. Hold for a count of 10.
2. Straighten up and twist to the other side, putting your left foot outside your right knee. Hold for a count of 10.

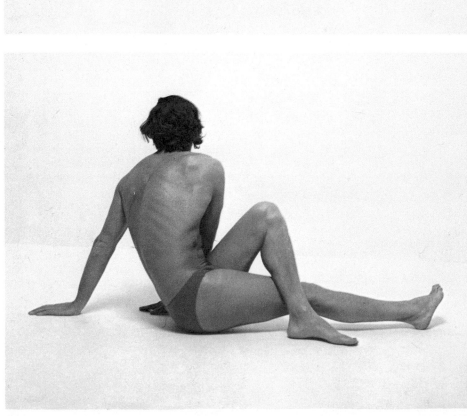

THE BOW—PREPARATION
Strengthens the muscles in the lower back, slims the thighs, increases the flexibility of the hip joints

1. Lie face down with your arms at your sides. Bend your knees and grasp your ankles. Raise your knees by pulling your feet towards your body. Do not raise your hips or head. Hold for a count of five.
2. Lie face down. Bend your right knee and hold your ankle with your left hand. Support your upper body with your right arm. Raise your right leg and look straight ahead. Hold for a count of eight.
3. Repeat with your left leg raised.

THE WINDMILL
Stretches and slims the waist and sides, massages all the internal organs

Stand with your feet well apart and link your hands above your head. Inhale. Turn your head, arms and trunk to the left and, as you exhale, make a half-circle with your straight arms. Smoothly continue the circle, inhaling as you move to the right. Come back to the starting position. Repeat twice, then circle three times in the other direction.

Relax your whole body. Breathing calmly, hang loose from your waist with your hands near the floor.

Lesson 9

As this course enters a more advanced phase it is well to bear in mind that one of the cardinal rules of the practice of *hatha* yoga is—do not strain. Yoga should make you more fit, more supple and more healthy, but it should never result in a strained or sore muscle or any physical discomfort.

If any of the postures prove difficult or you feel uncomfortable as you do it, do not try to complete it. Instead return to an earlier and less difficult stage of the same pose and build up gradually. The Cobra in this lesson, for example, is quite hard. If you cannot do it easily, go back to the first (or an earlier) Cobra and work through the variations, doing a new one each day or every two days. If, on the other hand, you find a new pose, such as Pushing-up, too difficult, then find a similar but more simple one in a previous lesson and practise that until the relevant areas of your body are supple enough to progress to the more advanced position.

Remember, too, that these postures are to be done only to the best of your ability. Relatively few people can achieve, say, a perfect Boat pose, and hold it for several seconds, until they have practised yoga for some time. This does not mean that doing a posture to a limited degree is pointless—the benefits still apply.

You cannot hurry yoga, either in learning to master a single pose or in progressing through a course. Both the approach and the movements are slow and graceful. Yoga is a gentle process, for the mind and the body must learn to adapt to new directions and applications. But, in the end, your patience will be richly rewarded.

This lesson, like the ones before, is designed for both men and women and should take about 30 minutes. As usual, begin by relaxing.

THE RELAXATION POSE
Lie on your back with your feet slightly apart, your arms at your sides, your palms facing upwards and your head and neck relaxed. Consciously feel all the little muscles in your face relax. Imagine that a hand is slowly stroking your hair and relaxing your scalp. As always, breathe only through your nose. Try to relax your mind as well as your body. Remain like this for two minutes before and after each yoga session.

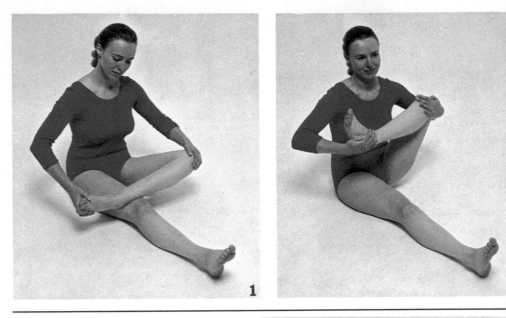

1

2

PUSHING UP
Strengthens back, arms and thighs, slims buttocks and thighs. The closer your feet are to your body the easier it is to do this exercise. Try to increase the distance as you practise

1. Lie on your back. Bend your knees and keep your feet flat on the floor. Put the palms of your hands on the floor parallel with your head. Inhale.
2. Holding your breath and keeping your head on the floor, press down with your hands and raise your body. Hold for a count of five. Slowly return to the floor and exhale.
Repeat twice.

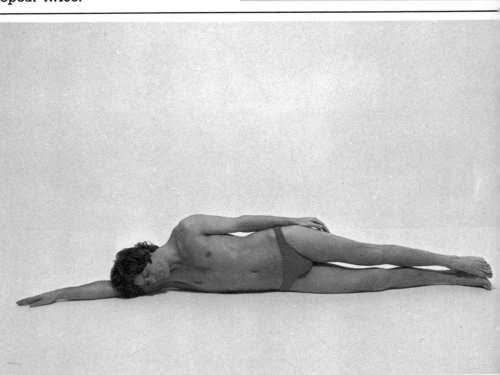

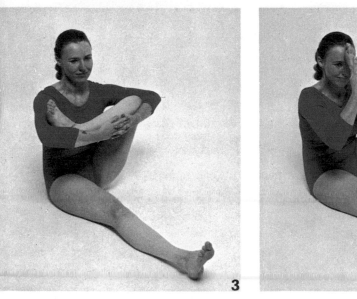

3

4

LEG EXERCISE–2
Flexes pelvis, knees and ankles

1. Sit with your legs out straight. Bend your left leg and rest it on your right leg, just above the knee. Hold your left foot with your right hand and, your ankle relaxed, circle it five times in each direction.

2. Hold the heel of your left foot and raise your left leg, gently circling it from the knee five times.

3. With your hands linked, cradle your left leg so that your left foot rests in the crook of your right arm and your left knee in the crook of your left arm. Move your leg from side to side.

4. Hold the lower part of your left leg with your hands and try to touch your forehead with your toes.

Repeat with your right leg.

1

2

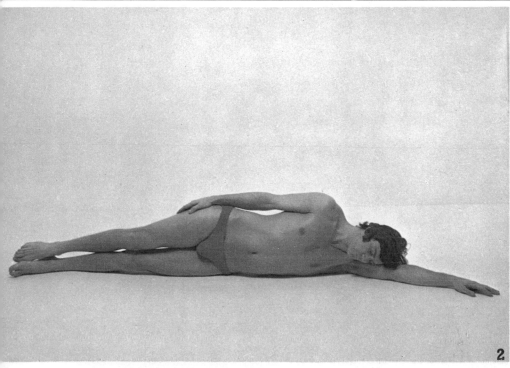

2

SIDE BREATHING
Improves breathing, relaxes

1. Lie on your right side with your head resting on your upper arm. Keep your feet together and lie straight. Inhale, concentrating on your left nostril and the whole left side of your body. Exhale.
Repeat nine times.

2. Lie on your left side and repeat the 10 breaths, concentrating on the whole right side of your body.

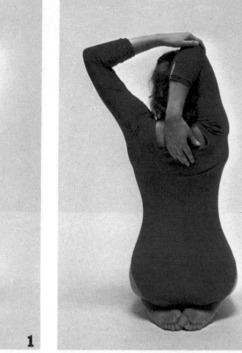

1

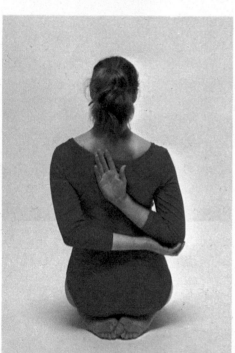

2

3

4

THE WARRIOR
Increases the capacity of the lungs, strengthens legs, chest, back and neck, improves balance

Stand with your feet together and your arms at your sides. Bend your left leg and put your right foot forward about four feet. Resting your weight on your right leg, bring your elbows up to shoulder height. Inhale deeply and pull your elbows as far back as possible. Without exhaling, hold for a count of five. Repeat with the left leg forward.

1

THE COW–PREPARATION
Increases suppleness of the arms and shoulders, strengthens the back

1. Sit on your feet in the Thunderbolt posture. Raise your right arm and bend it backwards so that the palm of your hand is against your upper back. Put your left hand on your right elbow.
2. Using your left hand, gently move your right elbow to the left and ease your right hand down as low as possible. Keep your head and back straight. Move your elbow backwards and forwards several times.
Repeat with your left arm.
3. Put your right arm behind your back so that the back of your right hand is against the middle of your back. Put your left hand on your right elbow.
4. Using your left hand, gently move your right elbow to the left and ease your right hand up as far as possible. Move your elbow backwards and forwards several times. Repeat with your left arm.

2

1

2

THE FULL SHOULDER-STAND
Increases circulation, improves suppleness of the spine and neck
This pose should not be done by people who have an over-active thyroid gland or during menstruation

Lie on your back with your arms at your sides. Bend your knees and slowly raise your legs to a vertical position. Pause for a count of five.
1. Swing your legs backwards towards your head, supporting your back with your hands.
2, 3. Rise up, supporting your back with your hands until your legs are vertical. Keep your chin tucked in and your back straight. Your weight should be on your shoulders, not on the back of your neck. Breathing calmly and abdominally, hold for a count of 15. Gradually increase this by a few seconds each day.

3

1

THE FISH
This is a counterpose for the Shoulder-stand and should always be done after this posture

Lie on your back with your legs together and your arms at your sides. Supporting yourself with your elbows, raise your upper body. Arch your back and drop your head back until it rests on the crown, sliding yourself forward on your elbows as you do this. Stretch your arms forward and put your hands on your thighs. Take three deep breaths. Put your elbows back on the floor. Slowly raise your head and then lie flat and relax.

1

2

THE DOLPHIN
Stimulates circulation, improves the complexion and balance

Sit on your feet in the Thunderbolt posture.
1, 2. Move forward on to your elbows and knees. To measure the proper distance from your hands to your shoulders, put your forearms next to each other and then move them forward, linking your hands to form a triangle.
3. Place your head between your linked hands.
4. Keeping your legs straight, move up on to your toes. Hold for five breaths.
Bend your knees and slowly return to the kneeling position. Then return to the Thunderbolt and relax.

3

4

THE COBRA–6
Expands the ribcage, strengthens the muscles of the stomach, chin, neck and back

Lie face down with your forehead on the floor, your hands next to your shoulders and your feet together. Place the palms of your hands against the back of your ribcage as high as possible. Bend your knees, and, keeping your feet together, pull your heels towards your body. Raise your head and shoulders and breathe deeply five times.
Add one more breath each day until you can hold the pose for 10 breaths.

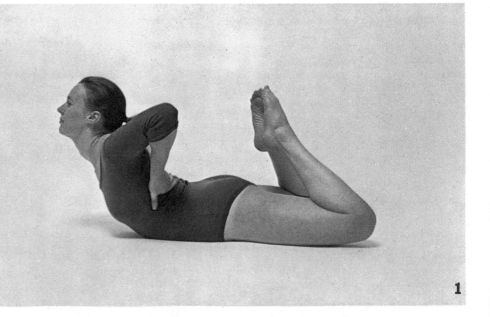

1

1

2

THE TRIANGLE–5
Strengthens leg muscles, increases the suppleness of the spine, slims the waist

Stand with your feet well apart and link your hands behind your back. Turn your right foot outwards and bend your right leg. Inhale. As you exhale, bend forward and touch your right knee with your forehead. Relax in this position for a count of five, then inhale and straighten up. Repeat with your left leg.
If you can touch your forehead to your knee with ease, then bend your right leg more and try to ease your head down as near to your foot as possible. Relax for a count of five, then inhale and straighten up. Repeat with your left leg.

HEAD CLEARING POSTURE
Relieves discomfort from blocked sinuses and nasal passage This posture is not included in the 30-minute daily programme. To be most beneficial it should be held for at least 10 minutes

Sit on your feet in the Thunderbolt posture. Cross your arms, putting your fingers under your arms. Close your eyes and press slightly inwards with your fingers. Breathe slowly and rhythmically. This exercise can be practised at any time, even after meals.

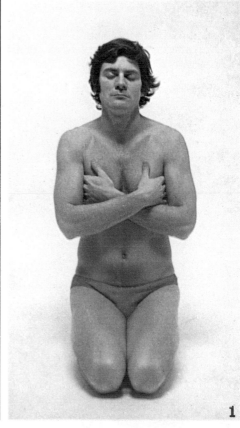

1

Lesson 10

Now that you have been doing your yoga exercises for at least two months, you should feel healthier and more supple. But you could well notice other changes in your life, too. Has your power of concentration improved? Have you become more aware of and sensitive to sounds, smells, colours, and to other people? The accumulation of such heightened experience can bring a radical change into your life, and help to make your life more positive and enjoyable.

Try this experiment tonight. Just before you go to sleep recount your day, but in the reverse. Be as exact as you can, not only in remembering what happened last, but also in going carefully through the next thing such as watching television, reading, what you ate for your last meal, what you did prior to that and so on during the whole day until you have reached the moment when you woke up. Then, and this is the most important part, check again to be sure that you have not left out anything by starting with the morning and going through the day. The part originally left out will indicate which experience your unconscious wants to avoid.

Look at your day objectively and unemotionally, as if you were watching a scene being enacted with you as a member of the audience. Then ask yourself, "What else could I have done? Did I take things too seriously and exaggerate them in my mind?" If you are capable of doing this sincerely, you have definitely advanced in yoga. You will then be able to rectify unpleasant experiences which otherwise act like a canker, eating deeper and deeper into your unconscious, making you feel miserable and dejected.

This lesson, like the previous ones, is designed for both men and women and should take about 30 minutes. As always, begin by relaxing.

You may like to try the breathing exercises and the Sun Worship sequence next. They are both excellent additions to your routine. Otherwise continue on to lesson 11 on page 80.

THE RELAXATION POSE
Lie on your back, feet slightly apart, arms at your sides, palms facing upwards and your head and neck relaxed. Close your eyes. As always, breathe only through your nose. Try to relax your mind as well as your body. Remain like this for at least two minutes before and after each yoga session.

1

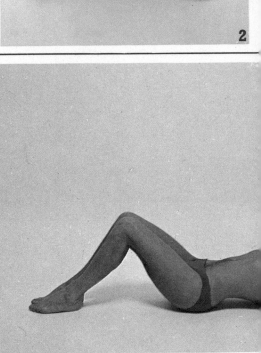

2

THE LEG STRETCH
Stretches the spine and hamstrings, flexes ankles and toes, corrects hollow back

1. Lie on your back with your arms outstretched above your head and, keeping your feet flat on the floor, bend your knees until you feel the small of your back touch the floor.
2. Raise your feet off the ground and gradually straighten your legs to a vertical position. Flex your ankles several times, trying to point your toes at your head. Keeping your legs still, make circles with your feet, moving them first in one direction and then in the other.
Bend your knees and bring your legs down gently to the floor, putting the soles of your feet down then pushing your legs forward.

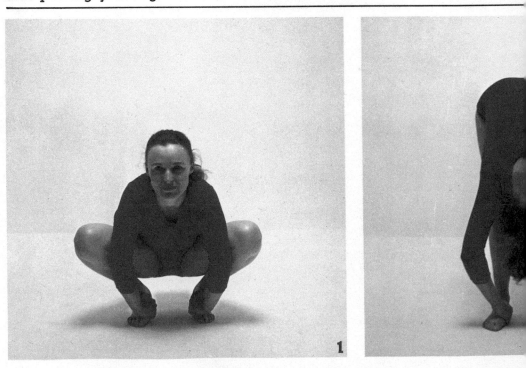

1

3

4

ONE-SIDED BREATHING
Improves breathing, massages the abdomen

1. Sit with your feet behind you and your knees wide apart.

2,3. Link your hands behind your back and bend to your left knee so that the left side of your chest rests on your thigh. Turn your head slightly so that your left nostril is closed. Take five deep breaths through your right nostril. Inhale and sit up.

4. Take three normal breaths and then bend to your right knee. With your right nostril blocked, take five deep breaths through your left nostril.

Inhale and sit up. Then take three normal breaths.

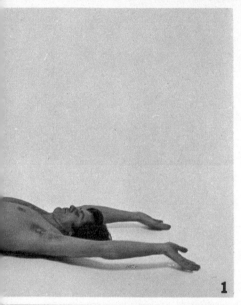

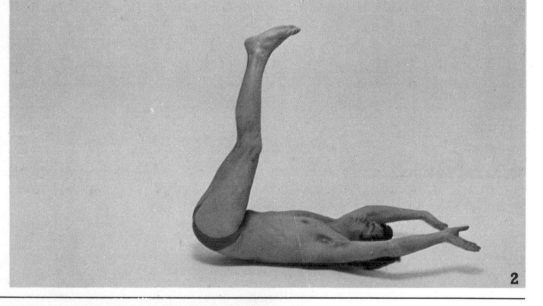

1

2

2

3

SQUATTING–2
Stretches neck, back and leg muscles, relieves constipation

1. Squat with your feet flat on the floor and about nine inches apart. Put your fingers under your insteps so that the palms of your hands are against the sides of your feet. Inhale.

2,3. Exhaling and still holding your feet, rise up gently until your legs are straight and your head is close to your knees. As you exhale pull your abdomen in. Hold for a count of three.

Return to the starting position while inhaling.

Repeat twice.

1

3

2

THE DYNAMIC CAT
Strengthens lower back, corrects hollow back, improves balance and breath control

1. Kneel with your hands directly below your shoulders, and your body parallel to the floor.
2. Inhale and, looking up, stretch your right arm and left leg as high as possible.
3. Exhale and, arching your back, bring your right arm down to the floor and your head down. Bend your left leg and take your left knee as close as possible to your nose. Return to the starting position. Repeat, stretching your left arm and right leg.
Repeat the whole exercise twice.

THE SHOULDERSTAND—2
Strengthens and stretches the spine, hips and hamstrings

First, adopt the full Shoulderstand position. Lie on your back, bend your knees and slowly raise your legs to a vertical position. Pause, then swing your legs back towards your head and rise up, supporting your back with your hands, until your body is vertical.

1. Keeping your right leg straight and vertical, allow your left leg to come down by its own weight until your toes touch the floor. Bring it up again to the previous position.

2. Keeping your left leg upright, allow your right leg to come down by its own weight until your toes touch the floor.

Repeat three times with each leg. Then lower both feet to the floor, trying to keep your legs straight. Lower your back and, keeping your knees bent and close to your chest, roll down to the starting position.

1

2

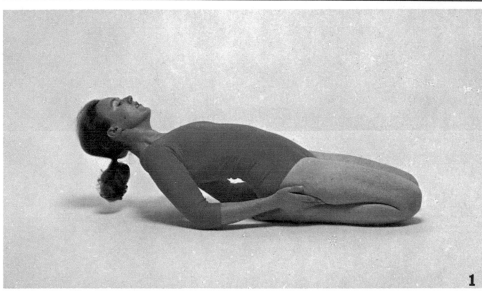

1

2

THE FISH—2
Stretches the thighs, strengthens the back
If this version proves difficult, practise the earlier example of the same exercise

1. Sit on your heels in the Thunderbolt posture. Lean backwards, supporting yourself first on one elbow and then the other. Arch your back.

2. Sliding your elbows forward, bend your head back until it rests on the crown. If you can, put your hands on the top of your thighs. Take three to five deep breaths. Bring your elbows back and, slowly raising your head, transfer your weight to your arms. Sit up in the Thunderbolt posture and relax with your eyes closed for a few seconds.

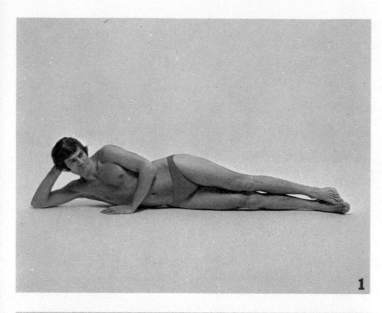

1

2

3

THE SIDE STRETCH–2
Strengthens the lower back.

First, lie in the side relaxation position on your right side, with your head resting on your right arm. Bend your left leg and put your left knee on the floor in front of you, and your left arm behind your back.
1. Support your head with your right hand and put your left hand flat on the floor in front of you. Straighten your left leg so that your legs are on top of each other.
2. Raise your feet and hold them about one foot off the floor for a count of five. Bring them down slowly.
Raise your legs again and, keeping them straight, move them backwards and forwards several times.
3. Lie on your left side and repeat.

THE BOW
Improves posture, massages the abdomen, strengthens the spine

Lie face down with your arms at your sides and your chin on the floor. Bend your legs and, keeping your knees slightly apart, hold your ankles or feet. The big toes should be touching. Keeping your arms straight and your toes together, raise your legs and then your head. Allow your feet to pull your arms up higher, so that your chest also leaves the floor. Bend your head back. Your feet should always be higher than your head. Hold for a count of six.

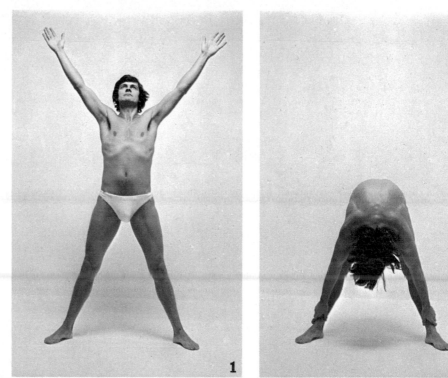

1

2

THE TRIANGLE—6
Stretches the whole body, slims the waist and stomach

1. Stand with your feet about three feet apart and your hands out stretched wide apart above your head. Stretch up and inhale to a count of two.
2. Exhale and swing down, touching your feet or ankles to a count of two.
Repeat nine times.

THE EAGLE
**Strengthens the leg muscles, improves balance and co-ordination
There are two versions of this posture, the static and the dynamic**

Twist your right leg around your left leg and, putting your right elbow under your left elbow, bring your hands together. Press both your arms and legs tightly together, and hold for a count of five. Repeat with your arms and legs reversed. From the first position bend your left leg and, trying to keep your body upright, lower your body as much as possible. Hold for a count of five and then rise up slowly. Repeat from the first position with your left leg wrapped around your right leg and your arms reversed.

Yogic Breathing—1

Correct, trained breathing is a great boon to the health of the body besides having a calming and soothing effect on the mind. It is an integral part of yoga and has been developed into a vast science.

These simple, easy-to-follow exercises, the first in a two-part series, show you how to breathe properly so that you can gain the maximum benefit from the air you inhale every day. By following the exercises in conjunction with the main yoga course you will find many new

and attractive qualities and resources.

Yogic breathing gives many wide-ranging rewards. Your complexion will have a new lustre and vitality. Your movements will be more rhythmical and flowing. Your heart becomes stronger. Your voice will achieve an added timbre so that the modulation of your speech patterns are more attractive to listen to.

Start the exercises at a level which you find comfortable. Increase the length of time you hold your breath and the

number of times you do an exercise only very gradually.

Set aside as much time as you can for your breathing session. 10 minutes at the beginning is ideal. It is a good idea to do them immediately after you go through your daily yoga postures. Never practise the exercises on a full stomach. Always wait at least two hours after a meal. Practise with your eyes open or closed as you prefer unless stated otherwise.

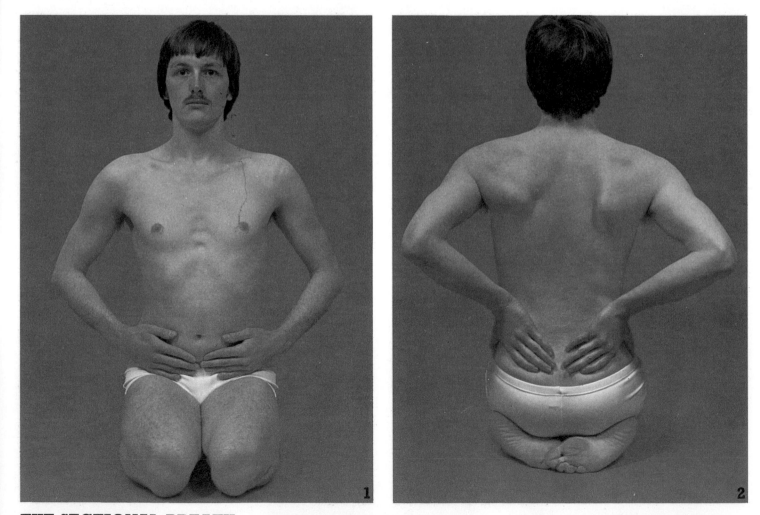

THE SECTIONAL BREATH
Calms the mind, corrects shallow breathing

Sit in the Thunderbolt posture (see lesson 4). Take six breaths in each of the following ways.
1. Place your hands lightly on your

abdomen and inhale. Exhale.
2. Now place your hands on your lower back and take six abdominal breaths.
3. Put your hands on your ribcage and inhale. Exhale. Notice how the distance between your fingertips differs when inhaling and exhaling.

4. Put your hands on the back of your ribcage and take six breaths.
5. Place your hands just under your collar bone and take six breaths.
6. Put your hands at both sides of the back of your neck and again feel your breath.

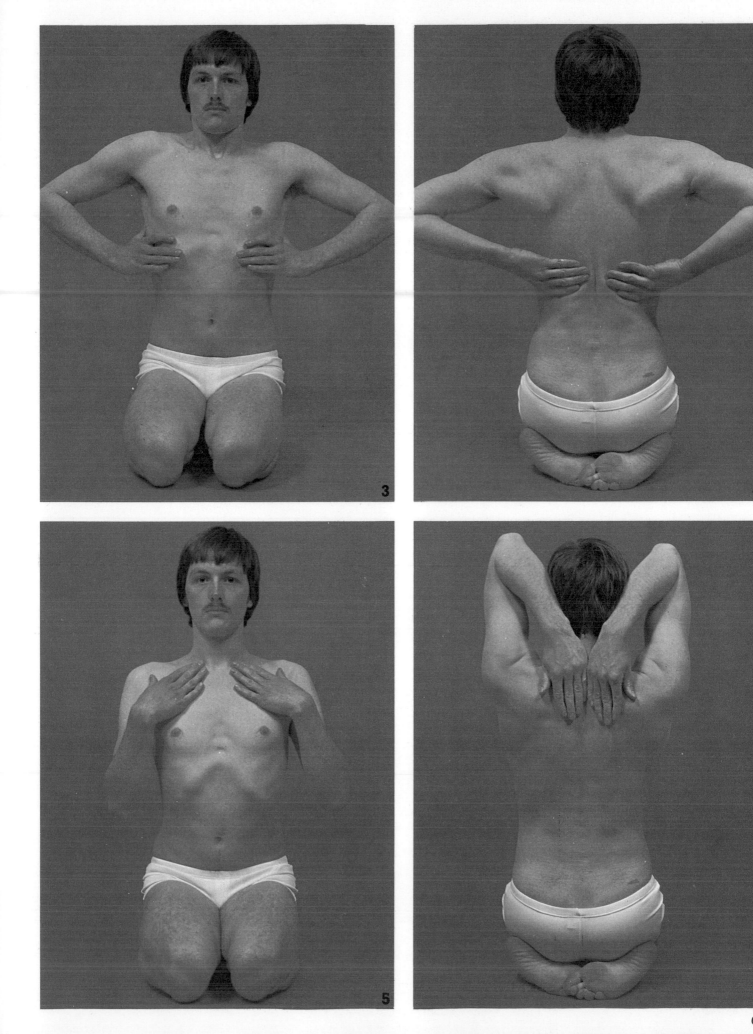

THE SNIFFING BREATH
Clears the nostrils

1. Close your right nostril with your thumb. Take little sniffs as if you are smelling a rose. These sniffs are only taken on the inhalation. When you feel that your lungs are full, exhale slowly and smoothly with your left nostril, still keeping your right nostril closed.
2. Close your left nostril with your index finger. Repeat the sniffing breath twice.

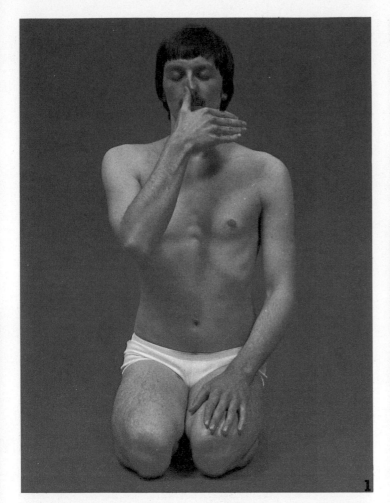

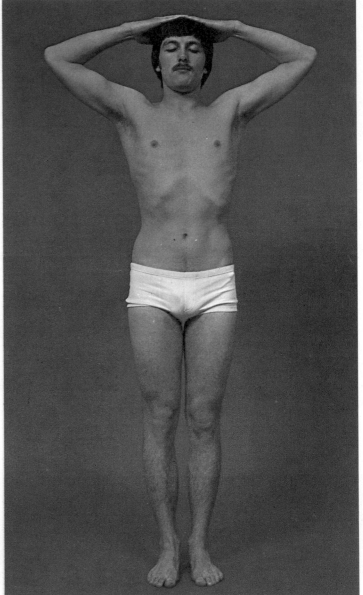

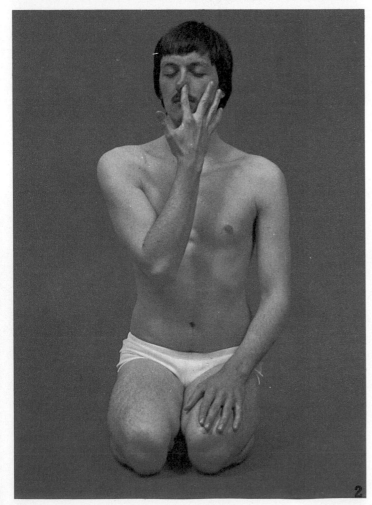

EXHALATION ON SOUNDS
Arouses vibrations through the body

Stand and close your eyes. Place both hands on top of your head. Inhale slowly and exhale in the same way, pronouncing the consonant SSS. Then inhale again and pronounce MMM on exhalation. Inhale once again and pronounce NNN on exhalation. Repeat the sequence twice.

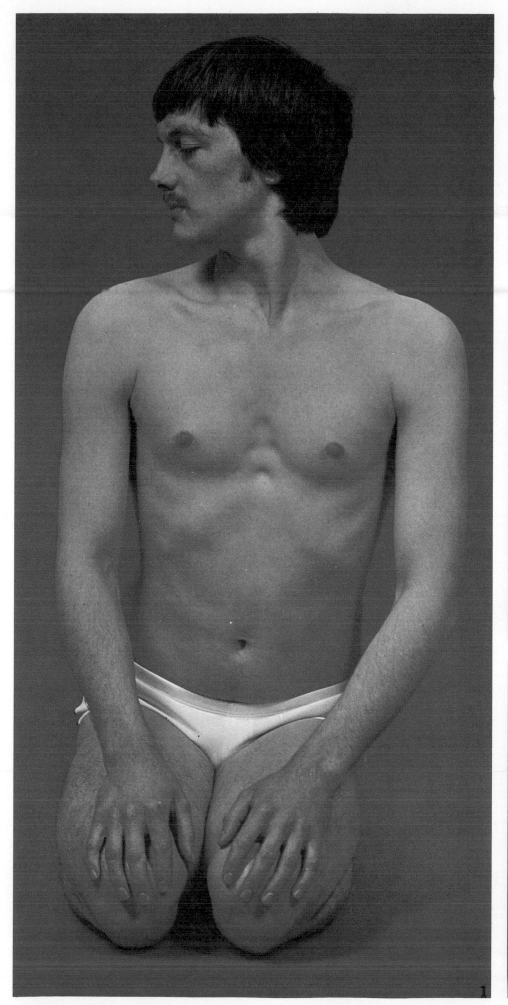

THE FOURFOLD BREATH
Relaxes the body, calms the mind

1. Sit in the Thunderbolt posture and inhale. Continue with the inhalation and at the same time turn your head to the right. Try to exhale with your right nostril only. This is difficult at the beginning but in time you will be able to do it. Slowly turn your head to the left and inhale at the same speed. Try to exhale with your left nostril only.
2. Return to the first position (face forward) inhale and bend your head backwards.
3. Exhale slowly while bending your head forward. Repeat the whole sequence twice.

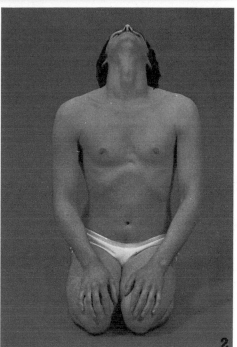

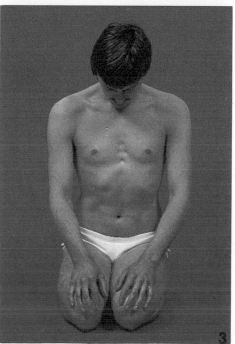

1

2

3

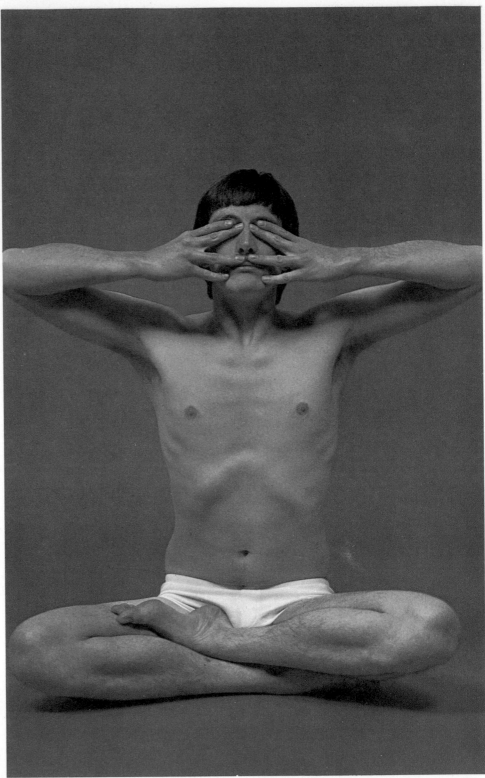

THE HA BREATH
Empties the lungs, relaxes the body

1. Inhale and stretch your arms and body as much as possible.
2. Uttering a sharp HA sound through the open mouth, bend forwards.
3. When you have exhaled to the full, relax with both palms on the floor. Repeat the whole sequence once.

THE BEE
Arouses vibrations at the back of the head, calms the mind

Sit in any comfortable posture. Close your eyes and put your first and second fingers over your eyes and your third and fourth fingers each side of your mouth. Inhale deeply and then exhale with a humming sound. Repeat four times. The exercise is very pleasant to do. It is a wonderful way of relaxing and soothing your mind at home or at work.

Yogic Breathing—2

The lungs are perhaps the most vital and important organ in your body. Their functioning affects your overall physical performance and well-being.

Correct breathing ensures that your lungs supply the other parts of your body with an abundance of pure, life-giving oxygen to keep you both healthy and lively. Anybody who has slipped into bad breathing habits will soon notice the vast difference these exercises make in providing a new zest. Tensions are removed, the body feels more relaxed, the mind is made calmer and the senses become sharper.

Skilled, artful breathing also gives you many benefits for your mind. It is an instant means of relaxation against the worries and tensions which can pre-occupy the mind and waste valuable energy.

The second part of the yogic breathing exercises help you to achieve a greater mental concentration and sharpness, giving you a new sensitivity when dealing with people or sorting out problems.

These exercises are designed to teach you the art of breathing in a simple, easy-to-follow way. And breathing is an art, not a function to be taken for

granted or allowed to fall into bad habits. Rather it should be consciously practised.

After practising the exercises for a few weeks you will notice a marked improvement in the way you inhale and exhale. Try to ensure that this carries on into your daily life and is not only confined to your practise sessions.

These exercises offer improved health and peace of mind. You will begin to notice many startling and pleasant benefits after a few weeks of practising. But these will not be gained without consistent, regular practice sessions.

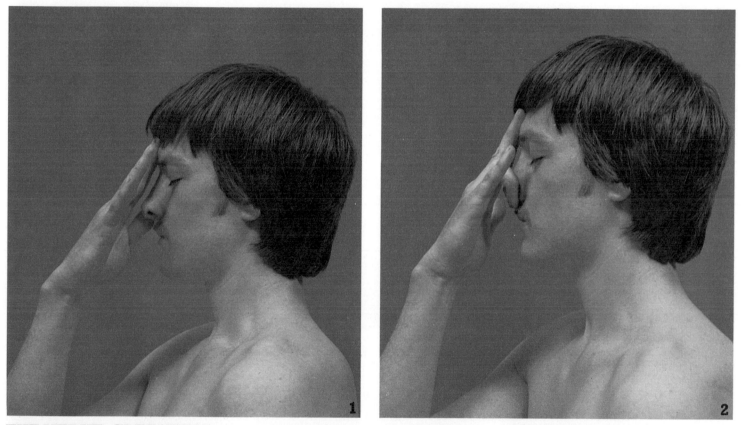

1

2

THE NERVE-CLEANSING BREATH

Soothes the whole nervous system, provides relaxation, gives a sense of well-being. This breath exercise is counted in rounds. One round consists of inhalation through the left nostril, exhalation through the right nostril, inhalation through the right nostril and exhalation through the left nostril. The length of inhalation and of exhalation can be equal when you start the exercise but as you get better exhalation should take twice the time. You will soon become aware what your own rhythm is but try to relate your

counting to the speed of your heartbeat. The exercise should be done with closed eyes.

1. Close the right nostril with your right thumb. Place your first and second fingers on your forehead. The ring and little fingers should not touch your face. Try to relax your hand as much as possible. Inhale.
2. Release the thumb and close the left nostril with your ring finger while exhaling. The two fingers on your forehead should remain immobile during the whole exercise and the little finger should never touch the face.
Alternate this inhaling and

exhaling for several minutes until you feel that your mind is at rest and peaceful.
After about a week of daily practise of this exercise, begin to relate your breathing to a mental count (such as three) for both the inhalation and exhalation. When you have perfected this double the time of exhalation. Do 10 rounds of this breath every day.
Use your left hand to count the rounds. Bend each finger, beginning with the thumb, counting two rounds on each finger. But it is up to you to find a method of counting which suits you best. Needless to say, all counting should be done mentally.

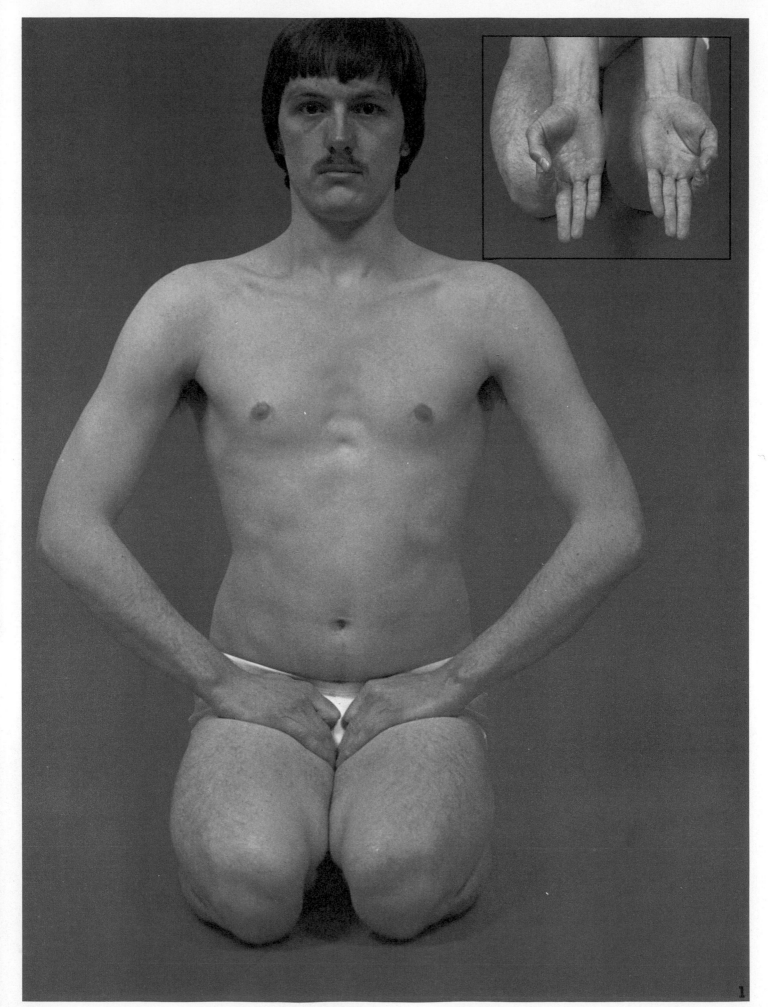

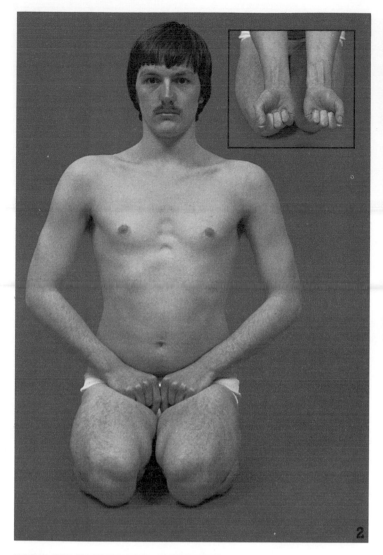

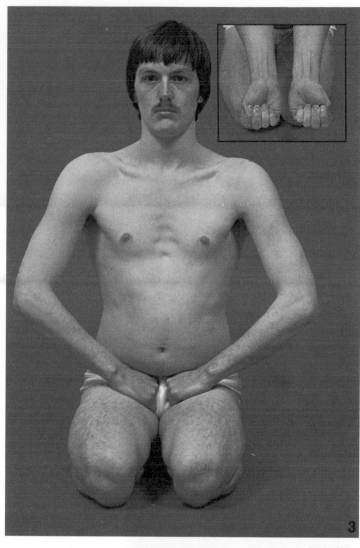

THE SECTIONAL BREATH

Calms the mind, increases air intake into the lungs, corrects shallow breathing.

This version of the sectional breath is carried out with the use of mudras, various positions for the hands and fingers. These give a new sensitivity when you breathe. Concentrate hard when going through the stages of this exercise—but only if you have been practising the original version for a few weeks. If you do not notice any differences do not be disappointed. They will soon come.

1. Sit in the Thunderbolt posture (see lesson 4). Place your hands in the Chinmudra by bending your index fingers so that they touch the tips of your thumbs—as shown in the insert picture.
Position your hands between your thighs so that your thumbs and index fingers touch your groin. Inhale from the abdomen. Then exhale. Repeat the whole breath five times.
2. This is done with the Chinmaya Mudra shown in the insert. Position your thumbs and index fingers as

before but curl up the other three fingers as well.
Place your hands into the groin and inhale thoracically (with the ribcage). Then exhale. Repeat the whole breath five times.
3. Make two fists with your thumbs inside your fingers. This is called the Adhi Mudra.
Place your hands into your groin. Inhale with the upper part of the lungs (shallow breathing). Then exhale in the same way. Repeat the whole breath five times.
4. Keep your hands in the Adhi Mudra and place them, knuckles against knuckles, on the navel. This is known as the Brahma Mudra. Inhale with the complete breath, drawing in the air by blowing out the abdomen then continuing the inhalation with the ribcage and extending it with the upper part of the lungs.
Then exhale in the same way when your lungs are full, slightly pressing the hands against the navel. Repeat the whole breath five times.
You can do this exercise with either closed or open eyes. But if your concentration is not too good close your eyes throughout. This will help you a great deal.

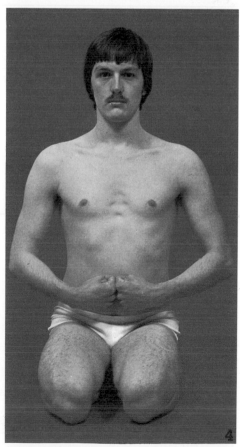

WALKING BREATH

Gives peace and serenity to the mind, helps concentration. This exercise is of special help for meditation and is used by Buddhist monks for this purpose. By walking and concentrating solely on the breath the mind becomes calm and contemplative.

Take three or four steps while inhaling. Try to be fully aware of your breathing.
Exhale taking the same number of steps or by doubling the number.

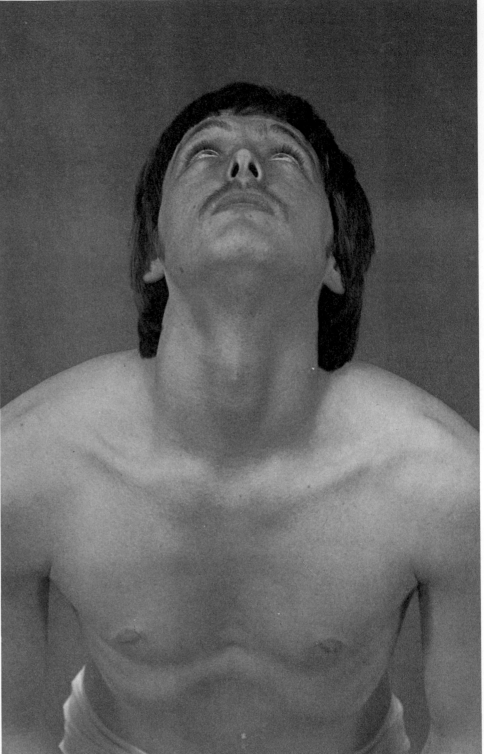

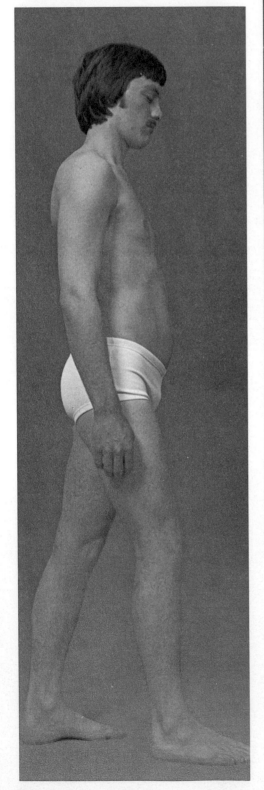

THE FAINTING BREATH

This is not an essential exercise but it is interesting and can be done at the end of your daily session. It should not be repeated. Keep your eyes open during inhalation and closed while exhaling.

Sit in one of the meditation postures—the Lotus, Half-Lotus or the Thunderbolt. Inhale slowly and bend your head backwards. Look up at the ceiling while you are inhaling and stretch the eye muscles as much as possible. Close your eyes and start exhaling while bending the head forward. Sit with your eyes closed and breathe normally.
You will notice a feeling of lightheadedness and giddiness after you have finished this exercise. For this reason be very careful when you are doing it. It can lead to fainting. When you have practised this exercise for some time try looking at the point between the eyebrows instead of at the ceiling, at first you will not be able to sustain this for long. But this will gradually disappear.

Sun Worship

Sun Worship is a neat, easy to follow "round" of exercises based on simple yoga positions. You can do it instead of other yoga courses, or in addition to them. The three minutes the exercises take—or the three-quarters of an hour if you repeat and lengthen them—are a wonderful method of loosening up ready to face the new day.

Sun Worship, called Surya Namaskar from the Indian words for Sun and Salutation, acts on the most important organs of the human body. And many people consider that repeating the postures a number of times a day is more than sufficient to keep them fit and well. Sun Worship improves the digestive system, and may help with constipation; it stimulates the nervous system yet at

A balanced and comprehensive sequence of yoga postures in an exercise which sets you up for each new day.

the same time calms and soothes; and it helps give you a clear skin.

Most important, Sun Worship revives and maintains a spirit of youthfulness. It's wonderful to know that you are ready to enjoy life and extract from it all it has to offer.

This group of exercises is a unit and must be performed as such. The best time to practise is in the morning before breakfast. Try to do it facing towards the East—to greet the rising sun. The main difference between Sun Worship and other yoga postures is that Sun Worship is performed quite quickly—once it has been properly learned.

The length of time can vary from three minutes to a quarter of an hour or more, depending on how you lengthen and repeat the postures. It's very important to lie down in the relaxed posture after a strenuous session, and to avoid getting cold you should cover yourself afterwards. Perform the exercise in the open air and you'll feel even better.

It's very important to concentrate fully on each movement, giving mental directions to the body to strengthen and shape the particular muscles involved in each posture.

Performing Sun Worship is a continuous process of learning: there's always the opportunity of learning more from these simple exercises and deriving increasing benefits. The first step, however, is to master the basic movements and to be quite sure of their sequence.

For the first week you try Sun Worship concentrate on learning the 12 postures, allowing enough time for full concentration on every single movement.

Practise the first four positions until your body knows them and then add one more and so on until you come to the last three, which are the reverse movements of the first three.

If you are not yet fully proficient at yoga, do not worry. It's unlikely that you'll be able to perform the postures to perfection for some time, but it's far more important to do them to the best of your ability *without straining*.

Few people, for example, will be able to put their hands flat on the floor beside their feet and at the same time bring their forehead to their knees for the third and tenth positions. At the beginning you should bend the knees slightly rather than straining the hamstrings and also touch the floor only with the fingertips. Be gentle with the forward bending movement. In a matter of weeks you'll be able to get both palms on the floor as a result of gently stretching your muscles and ligaments each day. Even so, never strain at this position—you can always bend your knees if you need to.

Once you have learnt the sequence and are quite sure of the postures you will find that you automatically perform them without having to stop and think what comes next: then the time has come to co-ordinate the postures with your breathing. Sun Worship is not only a physical "work-out" which increases

Position 1
Sets the tone for the whole exercise by calming the mind and collecting the necessary concentration.
Stand up straight with your feet together and place the palms of your hands together in front of your chest.

Position 2
Stretches and strengthens the abdominal and intestinal muscles, increases the suppleness of the spine, increases the capacity of the lungs.
Link your hands with your thumbs and raise your arms. Stretch upwards and then backwards as far as possible while inhaling deeply.

Position 3
Slims the stomach, improves circulation and digestion, stretches the hamstrings, increases the suppleness of the spine.
Swing forward while exhaling and try to get both hands flat on the floor outside your feet so that your fingertips and toes are on the same line and your forehead touches the knees. Don't strain in this position—it doesn't matter if your legs are slightly bent although the expert keeps the legs straight. Exhale and pull the abdomen in and up.

Having placed the hands in this position they should remain there throughout the exercise until Position 11.

circulation and acts on all the muscles and organs of the body; it can also be regarded as one long dynamic breathing exercise through which you increase the vital supply of *prana*, or the "life force", which you inhale. This life force or energy enables experts to repeat the exercise hundreds of times without feeling tired or getting out of breath.

You'll notice that in every movement which opens outward you take an inhalation whereas, when the body is bent inward, you exhale. Try from the beginning to breathe as deeply as possible from the abdomen and the whole of the thorax.

During each inhalation expand the chest as much as possible and open the body up to receive the air—feel that you are inhaling the life force. When you exhale, breathe out everything you want eliminated and pull the abdomen in and up (this does not apply to pregnant women). Naturally all breathing is done through the nostrils. And the Sun Worship will help to clear a blocked nose.

If you get breathless at the beginning this is caused by not breathing deeply enough or by performing either too fast or too slow; if you perform too slowly you tend to get "stuck" in certain positions and have to hold the breath in or out for too long so that the lungs may be strained. If your breathing is too shallow it indicates that not enough oxygen is inhaled to give your body the required

Position 4
Tones up the abdomen and pelvis, strengthens the thighs, legs and spine.
Thrust your right leg straight back with your right foot on the toes. When you start your knee can also touch the floor. Bend your left knee and bring the weight of your body forward so that most of it is supported by the left leg and stretch your back, arching it upwards with your head bent back. Depending on the length of your arms, your palms remain in their original position or are lifted so that only the fingertips remain on the floor. Inhale deeply and expand the chest as you look up.

Position 5
Strengthens the arms and legs.
Bring your left leg back and, with your arms and legs straight, make your whole body and head one straight line in the front support position. Hold the breath, and try to have your hands directly below your shoulders.

Position 6
Tones up the whole body.
Lower your body so that your toes, knees, chest and chin are touching the floor; your hips and buttocks are raised and your stomach should be off the floor. Your palms should be flat. Make sure that your elbows are bent so that your arms are close to your sides. Exhale.

energy and inhalations and exhalations become too violent. Ideally each breath should be as smooth as the whole performance.

With the Sun Worship you set your own pace. Once the basic postures and the combination with breathing have been mastered, you find your own rhythm.

You can tell when you have found your own ideal rhythm and pace—you will then be able to perform more repetitions without feeling tired or breathless. To begin with, five rounds may be the maximum but after a few weeks you will have increased it to 10 or 12. During the following relaxation you will notice that the circulation is increased but that your breath is hardly faster than at the beginning and that you are not tired. Indeed, you are full of renewed energy.

The classical form of the Sun Worship consists of a cycle (two rounds) which means that the right (or left) foot is put forward in positions four and nine (and not alternate feet as shown in our photographs); in the next 12 movements the other foot would be put forward. Either method is acceptable and it depends on which one you prefer.

Sun Worship should be practised in a warm but not overheated room which should be well ventilated. If you are pregnant and have been regularly practising yoga exercises you can continue with the Sun Worship up to the fifth month—

Position 7
Increases the suppleness of the spine, loosens the neck and shoulders.
Lower your body to the floor so that your feet are resting on the insteps. Go into the Cobra, which you have already learned, by raising your head, shoulders and chest. Inhale and look upwards, keeping your elbows bent and rising not further than your navel. Try to use your back muscles to draw you up.

Position 8
Stretches the hamstrings, strengthens arms and legs, improves the complexion.
Straighten your arms and, keeping your weight forward, raise your hips. Stand on your toes and slide the feet forwards slightly so that you can just stretch the heels down to put the soles of your feet on the floor. Drop your head between your arms and look at your thighs while exhaling.

Position 9
Strengthens and stretches the thighs, tones up the spine and abdomen.
Push your right foot forward between your hands so that your toes are once more in line with your fingertips. This is the same as Position 4 except that the other leg is brought forward. Inhale and stretch the back up as before.

if you feel comfortable. After the birth you should ask your doctor's advice if you can practise again. Sun Worship should be avoided during menstruation.

The History of Sun Worship
The Sun was worshipped in most ancient civilizations. People may not have carried out the same movements as in today's Sun Worship yoga, but they followed a simple ritual to pay respect to the heavenly host who gave them life by making fruit and grain grow and who warmed them. It is still practised in India by people living on the land—people for whom the daily rising of the sun is a meaningful occurrence.

The Rajah of Aundh, in the twentieth century, re-evaluated and improved the movements carried out by the peasants and brought Sun Worship to the consciousness first of his own countrymen and then of the world. After he had realized the benefits for himself and his country, he organized its introduction into schools and educational establishments. His book *The Ten Point Way to Health* (two movements were added later) was published in 1938.

Sun Worship is now generally accepted as part of *hatha* yoga, or physical yoga. Different teachers have made slight changes, but fundamentally the exercises fulfil the Rajah's aim: the natural physical movements mirror the cycle of human activity and revive a sense of being.

Position 10
This has the same effects and benefits as Position 3.
Bring your left foot forward to be in line with your right foot. Keeping your palms in the same position, raise your hips, straighten your legs and bring your head to your knees. Exhaling, pull your abdomen in and up.

Position 11
This has the same effects and benefits as Position 2.
As you inhale raise your arms and stretch them up with the thumbs linked, leaning backwards as far as possible.

Position 12
This has the same effects and benefits as Position 1.
Return to the first position as you exhale.
At the beginning drop your arms and stand relaxed, breathing deeply before starting on the next round. Later this will not be necessary and Position 12 will also represent Position 1 of the next round.

It is important that you do this series of exercises smoothly, moving from one position to the next at your own pace. Don't rush it, but don't linger too long. You'll soon find the right rhythm for you—and the Sun Worship will become a whole exercise which plays a vital role in your life.

12

10

11

Lesson 11

1

Some of you may have paused to learn the exercises in the special sections on breathing and Sun Worship, while others are continuing straight through to this lesson of the main yoga course. By this time, if you have been quite thorough in following the lessons, and have made sure that you have mastered the postures shown so far, then any expert would consider you well on the way to becoming proficient in Hatha Yoga.

It is difficult for some people to work on their own, without personal encouragement and moral support. On the other hand, you will already be aware of the benefits that you have gained in the course so far — increased poise, relaxation and better concentration, and this will help to spur you on to continuing with your routine. Following the lessons in this book is like going to your own, individual class every day in your own home.

Remember that the important thing is to do these postures to the best of your ability. Learning and mastering yoga is a gradual process—you'll only fool yourself by rushing it. If you find a particular posture or position difficult, keep practising the easier versions, or do it as best you can, until you become supple in that particular area. If you find your hamstrings are stiff, or your arms are weak, or your concentration is poor, then in addition to the normal course you should practise the exercises that improve these features.

Allow about 30 minutes a day for the exercises in this programme.

THE RELAXATION POSE
Lie on your back with your feet slightly apart, your arms at your sides, your palms facing up and your head and neck relaxed. Close your eyes. Put your tongue behind your lower teeth and relax your jaw. As always, breathe only through your nose. Try to relax your mind as well as your body. Remain like this for at least two minutes before and after each yoga session.

1

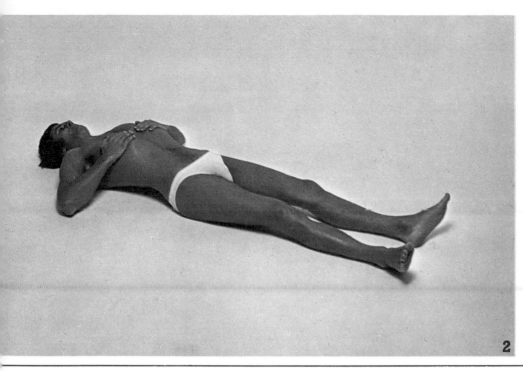

TOTAL BREATHING
Tones up the whole system, relaxes the body and calms the mind, increases the capacity of the lungs and volume of air intake

1. Lie on your back with your arms by your sides. Inhale abdominally by expanding your abdomen.
2. Then put your hands on your chest and inhale thoracically by expanding your chest. Draw up the air so your lungs are filled to capacity. Hold the breath for a moment and then start exhaling slowly. When your lungs are completely empty, pause and start the inhalation again.
Repeat nine times.

2

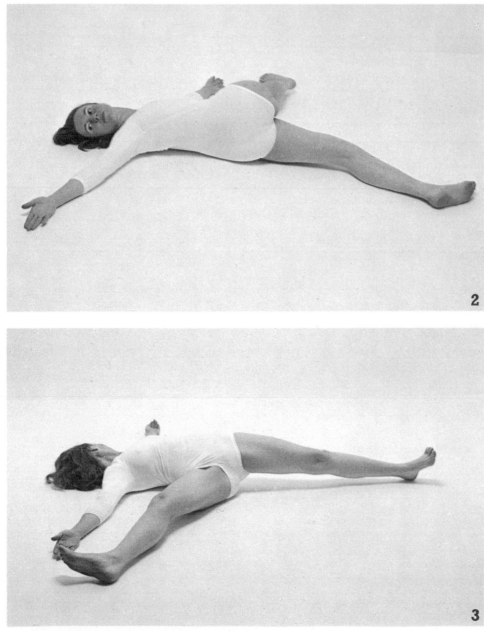

2

THE CROCODILE—7
Increases co-ordination and control, loosens lower back, strengthens the leg muscles, slims the waist

This exercise should be done slowly and smoothly, with the breath held throughout.
1. Lie on your back with your arms stretched out at shoulder height. As you inhale, raise your right leg to the vertical position.
2. Move your right leg slowly to the left until it touches the floor, at the same time turning your head as far as possible to the right.
3. Still holding your breath, raise your right leg and move it down to the right as far as possible, at the same time turning your head to the left.
Keep your arms straight and your left leg still throughout the exercise. Bring your leg back to the centre and lower it to the floor as you exhale.
Repeat with your left leg.
If this exercise is comfortable, repeat the movement again on the same breath.

3

CURLING UP—2
Strengthens the back, stomach and thigh muscles, decreases hollowness of the spine

1. Lie on your back with your legs straight and together and your arms crossed on your chest.
2. As you inhale sit up, first lifting your head and the top of your spine.
3. Come up until you are sitting with your back straight.
4. Start to come down again, keeping your head tucked in so that it touches the floor last. Exhale as you come down.
Repeat four times.

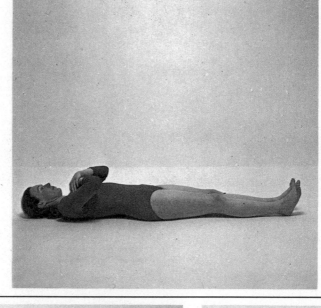

KNEELING UP
Strengthens the back and thigh muscles, improves balance and control

Use a cushion for your knees if the floor is too hard.
1. Sit on your heels in the Thunderbolt position and clasp your hands behind your head.
2. As you inhale, rise up slowly, keeping your head still and your back straight, until you are upright.
3. Return to the Thunderbolt as you exhale. Again move as slowly as possible, controlling the movement with your legs.
Repeat four times.

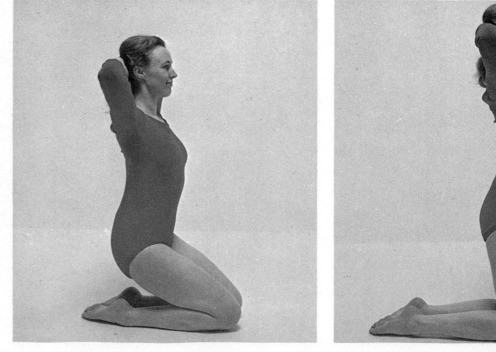

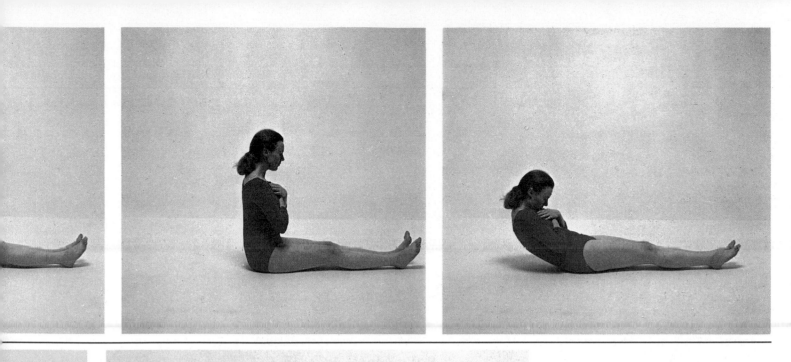

THE PERUVIAN MUMMY
Increases suppleness of the spine, stimulates the internal organs and the circulation of the blood, improves general fitness

This exercise should be done slowly and on a soft carpet or rug.
1. Lie on your back with both legs bent and your hands linked round your knees.
2,3. With your knees close to your chest, rock forwards and backwards 10 times, keeping your chin tucked in and trying to get the soles of your feet on the floor when you are upright.

THE SHOULDERSTAND—3
Stretches waist and hips, slims waist, stimulates the thyroid gland, improves the complexion and the condition of the scalp

1. Come up into the full Shoulderstand (see Lesson 9).
2. Keeping your neck and shoulders in the same position and your back supported by your hands, twist round to the left. Do not strain.
3. Twist round to the right. Repeat twice, then breathe abdominally for a few minutes. Come down slowly into the Plough (see Lesson 8).

THE PLOUGH—2
Stretches the spine, strengthens leg muscles, stretches hamstrings, reduces fat on the abdomen, improves breath control

Go into the Plough with your legs straight and together, your toes touching the floor, and your hands supporting your back. Take five abdominal breaths. Slowly move your feet apart as far as possible and try to place your arms on the floor. Hold for five breaths. Slowly return to the first Plough position.

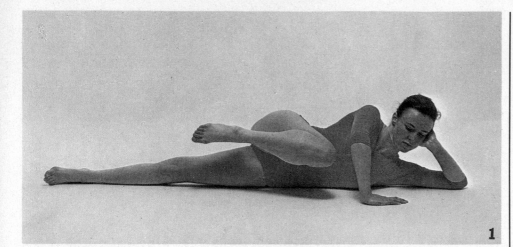

1

2

3

Lying on your front with the support of your elbows (as in the Cobra breathing below) is both relaxing and good for the spine. Use this position (and similar ones) whenever you can, particularly when you're reading on the floor or your bed. This posture also brings relief if you suffer from asthma.

COBRA BREATHING
Stretches the spine, improves circulation, loosens the back, strengthens neck muscles

1. Lie face down with your hands linked in front of you. Inhale and lift your head and shoulders looking up.
2. Exhale and, keeping your shoulders up, bring your head down to touch your hands. Keep your back completely relaxed.
Repeat five times.

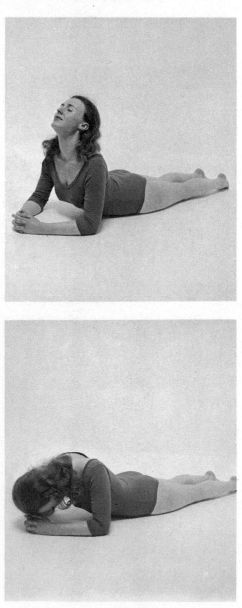

4

5

SIDE POSTURES
Strengthens the hips and lower back, stretches the thighs, alleviates constipation,

Lie on your left side in the Side Relaxation posture, your head resting on your outstretched left arm. Put your right arm behind your back and your right knee on the floor in front of you. Keep your left leg straight.
1. Support your head with your left hand and put your right hand flat on the floor in front of you as a balance. Raise your right leg, bend your knee, and bring it forward.
2. Move your right leg back as far as possible, leaning slightly forward to balance yourself.
Repeat this movement twice.
3. Raise your left leg and bend your knee so that both legs are together off the floor.
4. Bring both legs forward as far as possible, keeping them off the floor.
5. With your knees together, take your legs back as far as possible, leaning slightly forward to balance. Repeat the last two movements twice. Straighten your legs, bring them back to the ground, and return to the Side Relaxation pose.
Repeat the whole exercise lying on your right side.

THE TRIANGLE—7

Stretches and slims the waist and the back of the legs, stretches the hamstrings, loosens the shoulders

Stand with your feet well apart. Raise your arms sideways to shoulder height. Inhale. Lean forwards and exhale, twisting your body slightly to the left until your right hand is flat on the floor. Hold your left arm in a vertical position to form a straight line with your right arm. Relax in this position and take five deep breaths. Stand up and repeat with your left hand on the floor.

Lesson 12

Few of us live in areas where the air is clean. As a result we tend automatically to breathe in a shallow way (and often through the mouth) for fear of taking in too much dirt from the air. This is wrong: the human nose is a remarkably advanced filter, preventing most impurities from reaching the lungs and moistening and warming the air taken in. If you breathe through your mouth your body receives dry, cold, unfiltered air.

Many of you will have mastered the special exercises featured in this book which have been designed to make breathing through your nose an automatic reaction, to increase the capacity of your lungs, and to improve the efficiency of your whole cardio-vascular system.

If your nose is often blocked up through colds or sinus trouble try the *Cleansing Posture* in Lesson 9. Another successful method is *neti*, an Indian cure which uses a special can. You can do it, however, with a teapot with a thin spout.

Half fill the pot with lukewarm, slightly salted water, then bend your head over a basin or bowl. Relax your face and keep your mouth slightly open. Bend your head to the left and slowly pour water into your right nostril; if your mouth is open and your face properly relaxed, the water should come out of your left nostril. Repeat on the other side and then bend your head backwards and, with your mouth still open and your face relaxed, pour the water into your right nostril. This time you should spit the water out. Then repeat the whole sequence with the left nostril.

Exhaling, of course, is an important as inhaling. As children most of us are told to inhale deeply—but exhalation is never mentioned. It's the exhalation which gets rid of the toxins in our bodies. This too is also demonstrated in the special breathing course. Meanwhile, try to concentrate on breathing deeply and evenly through your nose, and become aware of the exhalation.

As usual, we recommend that you make sure that you have been very thorough with your exercises — if necessary repeat some of the postures which you find difficult, starting with the easier variations.

THE RELAXATION POSE

Lie on your back, feet slightly apart, arms at your sides, palms up and head and neck relaxed. Feel all the little muscles in your cheeks relax. Imagine that a hand is slowly stroking your hair and relax your scalp. As always, breathe only through your nose. Try to relax your mind as well as your body. Do this for at least two minutes before and after each session.

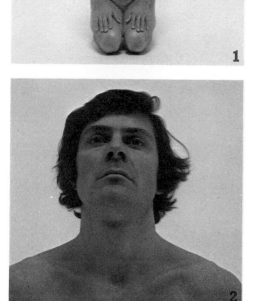

FLARED NOSTRIL BREATHING
Improves breathing, strengthens the small muscles in the nostrils, increases concentration, relaxes

Sit on your heels in the Thunderbolt posture with your hands on your knees. Breathe normally and flare the nostrils with each inhalation. Concentrate on the nostrils and sit like this, breathing slowly, for three minutes.

CROCODILE—8
Strengthens the hips, abdomen and lower back, develops co-ordination and control, counteracts acidity and constipation

Do this exercise as slowly and smoothly as you can.
1. Lie on your back with your arms stretched out at shoulder height. Inhale, slowly raising your legs to the vertical position. Hold the breath.
2. Move your legs slowly down to the right until they touch the floor, at the same time turning your head as far as possible to the left. Then raise your legs up to the centre again.
3. Move your legs slowly down to the left until they touch the floor, turning your head as far as possible to the right. Raise your legs back to the upright position.
Repeat the last two movements if you can still comfortably hold your breath. Otherwise bring your legs down to the floor again as you exhale. Keep your arms still throughout the exercise.

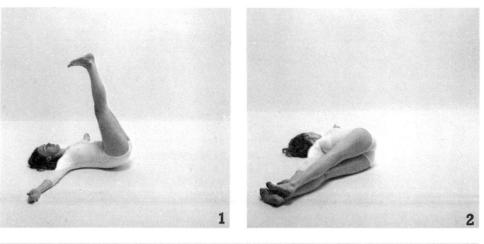

1

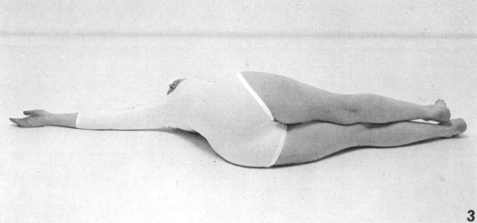

2

3

2

3

5

6

THE BACK STRETCH—6
Stretches and slims the hips and waist

1. Sit with your right leg stretched out as wide as possible and bend your left leg, putting your heel against your groin. Inhale and raise your arms above the head.
2. Bend slowly sideways towards the right leg, exhaling as you go down. Keep facing front. Do not twist or lean back or forward.
3. Come down as near to the right foot as possible and let the weight of your left arm bring you down a little further. Relax in this position and take three breaths. Inhale and return to the upright position.
4. Sit up with your left leg stretched out and bend your right leg, with the heel against your groin. Inhale and raise the arms above the head.
5. Bend slowly sideways towards the left leg, exhaling as you go down. Keep facing the front.
6. Come down as near to your left foot as possible. Relax in this position and take three breaths. Inhale and return to the upright position.
Repeat once.

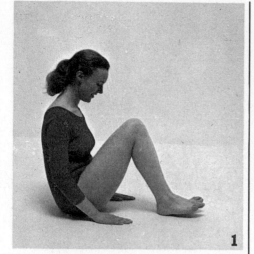

1

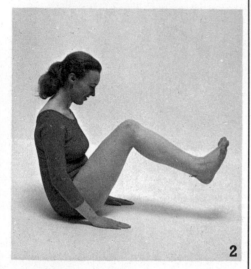

2

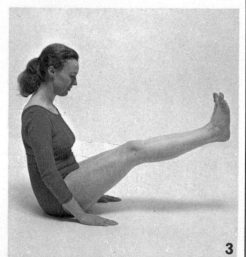

3

LEG RAISING
Strengthens the lower back and stomach muscles, develops balance

1. Sit with your knees bent and place your palms on the floor.
2. Lift your feet about a foot off the ground, keeping your back straight.
3. Straighten your legs and hold the pose for three breaths.
Bend your knees and bring your feet slowly back to the floor.
Repeat once.

THE CROW WALK
Firms and strengthens calves, knees, thighs and Achilles tendons. This is a good preparation for the Lotus

It should be done with the soles of your feet on the floor, squatting as low as possible, but if you cannot do this you can do it on slightly raised toes.
Squat as low as possible with your hands on your knees. Walk around or across the room in this posture. Count your steps and increase the number from day to day.

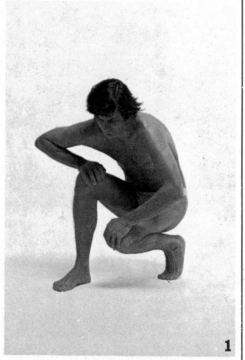

1

2

THE FROG
Strengthens the pelvis, firms the buttocks, relaxes the mind

Sit in the kneeling posture and put your knees apart as far as possible. Let your big toes touch behind so that your buttocks are on the floor, and place your hands on the knees. Keep your back, neck and head straight. Inhale and hold the breath to a count of five, then exhale slowly. Repeat the breath five times in this posture.

THE SHOULDERSTAND—4
Strengthens the hips and thighs, develops co-ordination and control, massages abdomen

1. Come up into the full Shoulderstand (see Lesson 9).
2. Bring your knees down together to your left shoulder, keeping your head, neck and shoulders in the same position and still supporting your back with your hands. Hold for a count of five.
3. Bring both knees down to touch your right shoulder. Remain for a count of five, then take your legs up. Repeat twice.
Return to the full Shoulderstand, then the Plough (Lesson 8).

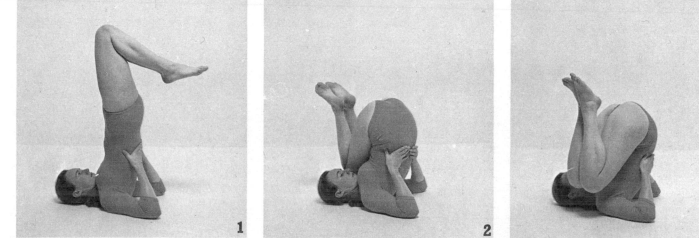

1

2

3

THE PLOUGH—3
Stretches the back muscles, relieves tension in the neck, tones up the hips and waist

1. From the Plough posture place your arms on the ground and walk on your toes as far to the right as possible. Keep the head still.
2. Walk round on your toes back to the centre and then to the left as far as possible. Walk back to the centre again. Slowly bring your feet down, with your legs bent, until your legs are on the floor.

COBRA—7
Strengthens the muscles in the small of the back, stretches the neck and thighs. Massages and slims the abdomen, increases awareness of breathing

Lie on your abdomen with your forehead on the floor. Place your hands palms downwards at waist level with your arms parallel to your body. Raise your feet, bending your knees. Slowly raise your head, shoulders and chest, stretching forwards. Inhale as you come up and pause when you are as high as possible. Return again slowly, bringing your forehead back to the floor last.

Repeat three times, then lower your feet to the floor and relax.

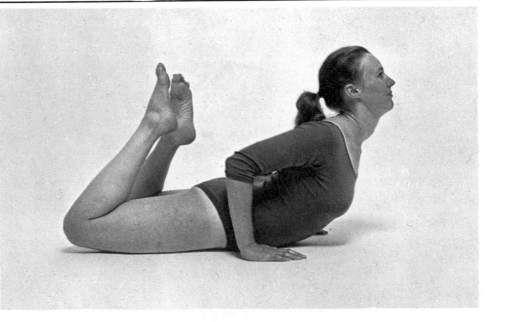

THE CRANE
Improves the complexion, circulation and balance, strengthens neck and arm muscles

1. Place the crown of your head on a cushion and put your palms on the floor about a foot below your head so that they are parallel and your elbows are bent. Rise up on your toes.
2. Slowly walk towards your hands until your weight is almost supported by your head, then raise your knees and balance them just above your elbows, crossing your ankles. Remain in this position for a count of 10.

To return, gently lift your knees and place your feet back on the floor. Kneel down in the Pose of the Child (see Lesson 6) with your forehead on the floor and both arms, palms upwards, by your sides. Relax like this for a minute and then, when you raise your head, come up very slowly. This exercise is easy to do providing that your weight is placed forwards before you go up on to your knees.

1

2

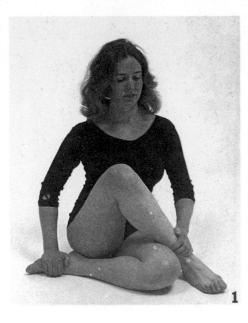

1

2

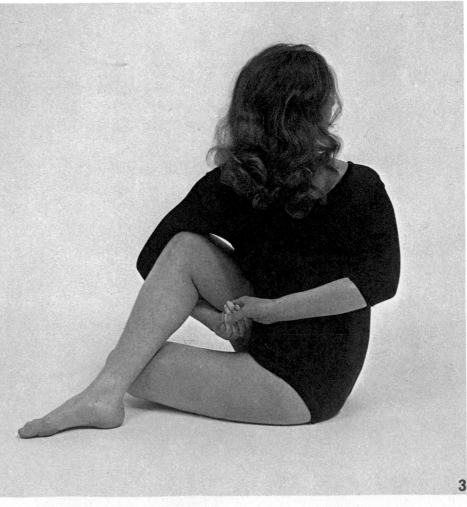

3

THE SPINAL TWIST
Massages and stretches the spine, slims the waist, relieves tension, strengthens eyes

1. Sit with your legs straight. Bend your left knee and place the heel as close to your right thigh as possible. Bend the right knee and place your right foot on the floor outside your left knee.

2. Bend the right arm behind your back, with the palm of your hand facing outward.

3. Put the left arm through the gap under your right knee, and hold your right hand with your left hand. Turn your head as far as possible to the right, keeping the spine upright, and look to the right as far as possible. Remain in this posture for five breaths. This posture is shown from a different angle in the picture on the opposite page.

Release your hands and relax, then repeat this posture in the opposite direction, your left leg over your right and your right arm under your left knee.

THE TREE
Develops poise and balance, strengthens leg muscles

Stand with your feet together. Put the sole of your left foot against the inside of your right thigh as high as possible, and raise both arms to shoulder height. Focus your eyes on a point straight ahead. Hold this posture for five breaths, and then close the eyes and hold it for a further five breaths.
Repeat with your right foot.

You've probably found out already that yoga both helps you to enjoy life and is itself enjoyable.

You gain a lot of satisfaction in yoga from the feeling you're improving—as well as the feeling of serenity and well-being that each session induces.

When there are two of you, progress is that much quicker. You can each see how close the other is to the right position and give a little help when it's needed.

And it's surprising how fast you will improve with a bit of encouragement.

Together you can judge which stage of the course is right for your level of ability, arrange that you'll repeat one programme for two or three weeks because you find you both enjoy it, or decide that you're ready to move on to the next stage.

Lesson 13

The main course continues with this lesson. As with the preceding lessons it's a complete routine in itself, a routine carefully planned to extend your ability at yoga.

Some of the exercises are new, some are variations or extensions of earlier poses, and some will already be familiar from previous lessons. This combination —something new, something familiar— adds up to a complete and logical routine. Practising it is another important step on your road to the mastery of physical yoga. This programme is a natural progression from lesson 12. If you have already learned and practised the poses for the Sun Worship sequence, that's fine. They are valuable in themselves, and provide an attractive variety of approaches to yoga. This widens your knowledge and physical control and increases your enjoyment of yoga.

The routine, though part of the course, stands by itself. Do it each day for a week —30 minutes a day is all it takes—and you will be ready to move on to the next part. But if you want to stay with this programme for longer, then do so. In yoga you move at your own pace.

As always, start with the relaxation pose and then move through the other exercises in order.

THE RELAXATION POSE

Lie on your back with your feet slightly apart, your arms at your sides and your palms up, your head and neck relaxed. Close your eyes and, as always, breathe only through your nose. Concentrate on relaxing in this position for several minutes before and after each yoga session.

THE WHOLE DYNAMIC BREATH

Increases breath control and increases the capacity of the lungs

As in the Whole Breath in lesson four the breathing is done in three stages: abdomen, ribcage and upper chest.

Begin in the Pose of the Child (see lesson six) kneeling on your heels with your forehead on the ground and your arms by your legs, palms facing up.

1. Start to rise up and, as you raise your arms until they are parallel with the ground, breathe into your abdomen. Raise your arms further and fill your ribcage with air. Finally fill the upper lungs and lean back with your arms behind your head.

2. While still leaning back bring your arms down until your hands touch your thighs. Then raise them. Slowly reverse the process, breathing out first from the upper lungs, then from the ribcage and finally from the abdomen. Return to the Pose of the Child.

Repeat the whole exercise twice.

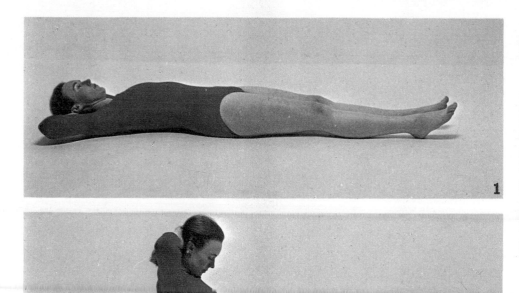

CURLING UP—3
Strengthens the abdomen and neck muscles

1. Lie on your back with your hands clasped behind your head.
2. Slowly begin to sit up, inhaling and curling the spine, first raising the head. Try to raise the vertebrae one after the other.
3. Complete the inhalation when your body is straight, and look up. Start exhaling as you come down. Uncurl your spine down from the lower vertebrae, tuck your head in and make sure that it is the last part of the body to touch the ground. Repeat the whole exercise twice.

Enjoy your yoga—and let it influence the whole of your life. The 30 minutes a day you give to your yoga routine soothes you so you feel ready for anything the day might bring. And more than that, the calm approach of those 30 minutes can bring benefits if you apply it to any of your problems.

THE BOAT
Strengthens abdominal and back muscles

1. Lie on your back. Inhale. Raise your head, shoulders and legs, keeping your arms and legs straight. Your head, hands and feet should be on the same level and not more than six inches from the floor. Hold for a count of 10.
2. Exhale and relax back to the floor.
Repeat once.

1

2

THE BALANCE—2
Stretches the hamstrings, tones up the thighs, improves balance and co-ordination

1. Sit with your knees together. Raise your feet off the ground and hold them just below the toes.
2. Still holding your feet, slowly raise your legs until they are straight. Then spread your legs as wide apart as possible, still holding your feet. Try to straighten your knees and balance on your buttocks. Remain in this position for three breaths. Then return to the second position, bend your knees and lower your feet to the floor. Repeat once.

1

THE MONUMENT
Makes the spine supple, strengthens the arms, improves balance.

1. Lie on your front with your hands under your shoulders. Bend your right knee, raise your left leg and support it by placing the knee on the sole of your right foot.
2. Lift your body by pushing up with your hands. Straighten your arms and look up. Take three breaths in this posture.
Slowly come down by bending your arms so that your chest comes down to the floor first. Glide along the sole of your right foot with the calf of your left leg and bring your right leg and then your left leg down to the floor.
   Repeat with your left leg bent and your right leg raised.

2

THE SHOULDERSTAND—5
Stretches the thighs, increases the flexibility of waist and hips

Come up into the Full Shoulderstand (see lesson nine). Bend your knees and point them at the ceiling, keeping your body straight. Twist your waist and legs to the left, keeping your knees upright. Then twist your waist and legs to the right, keeping your knees upright. Support your back with your hands and keep your head and shoulders steady on the floor throughout.
Repeat twice each side.
Straighten up into the Full Shoulderstand and then come down gently into the Plough, with your arms on the floor and your feet behind your head.

THE PLOUGH—4
Stretches the muscles of the upper back, tones up the spine

Stretch out your legs in the full Plough (see lesson eight).
1. Bend your knees and place them on the floor each side of your head. Put your hands on the back of your legs just above your knees. Remain like this for three breaths.
2. Support your back again with your hands and place both knees to the right side of your head.
3. Place your knees to the left side of your head.
Come back to the first position and relax for three breaths.
Slowly come down from the Plough.

1

2

3

THE RAISED BOW
Alleviates tension in the back muscles, increases concentration and body control

Position yourself on all fours. Place your left forearm on the floor in line with your shoulders, your palm down. Position your right knee carefully as the weight will be distributed between your right leg and your left arm. Grasp your left ankle with your right hand, raise your left leg as high as possible, and look up. Hold for a count of five, then slowly come back to the starting position.
Repeat with your right arm on the floor and your left hand clasping your right leg.

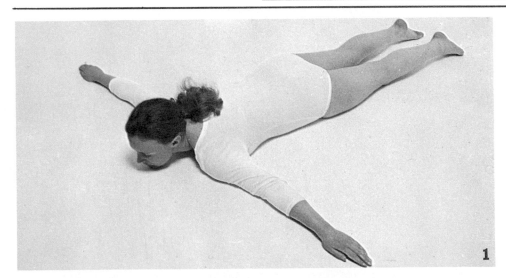

THE CROCODILE—9
Gives a gentle corkscrew movement to the spine, working particularly on the cervical vertebrae.

1. Lie on your front with your arms stretched out at shoulder height and your feet slightly apart. Rest your face on the chin. Inhale.
2. Slowly move your hips and legs to the right, at the same time turning your head to the left. Turn your head to the right side and at the same time twist your hips and legs to the left.
Repeat once to each side. Then exhale and return to the first position. Relax in the abdominal resting posture.

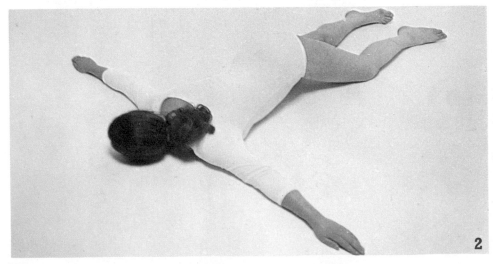

Every one of the individual yoga lessons is a complete routine in itself. And each is planned to give you a variety of poses that will match your natural rhythms as you move through them.
Always start a yoga session with the *relaxation pose*, this allows your mind and body to detach themselves from the day's rush and tumble.
Then move through the poses in the order we show them— you will find that quite naturally you are using different sets of muscles.

1

2

THE HALF LOCUST
This is the preparation for the Full Locust, working on the lumbar region and kidneys

1. Lie on your abdomen with your chin on the floor. Keep your feet together and your arms straight by your sides. Contract the muscles in the small of the back on the right side and lean on your right arm. Raise your right leg straight, trying to keep your left side relaxed. Hold for a count of five and slowly bring your leg down.
2. Repeat with your left leg.

THE MOVEMENT
Strengthens the leg muscles, improves balance and control

A. Stand with your feet about three feet apart and stretch your arms out at shoulder height. Inhale. As you exhale turn your head to the right and bend your right knee, turning out your foot to do so. Point your hands strongly. Inhale and come up to the centre again.

Then, as you exhale, turn your head to the left and bend your left knee. Do this exercise as slowly as possible in one continuous movement, repeating five times to each side.

B. Stand with your feet about three feet apart and raise your arms above your head with your palms together. Inhale. As you exhale twist your trunk to the left and bend the left knee turning out your left foot to do so. Look up between the palms of the hands. Inhale and come up to the centre again. Exhale and repeat on the right side, bending the right knee.

Repeat five times to each side, moving as slowly as possible. This is an extension of the Triangle in lesson five.

Lesson 14

The Lotus is the position most people who take up yoga are anxious to learn. They think of it as the queen of yoga positions and the most important one. The Lotus may be the queen—that's a matter of opinion—but all the positions are equally important. It's how you do the poses that counts. The Lotus is essential only for prolonged meditation; you can meditate for shorter periods in any comfortable sitting position.

It nevertheless has advantages. For one thing sitting in Lotus is a good way to sit and relax because your back has to be straight. Good posture brings many benefits. Above all, perhaps, is the fact that it's a beautiful pose. And it's worth mastering for that alone.

You may find it very easy if you can just fold your legs over without straining. But for most people it has to be a gradual process and one that shouldn't be rushed. If you find the Half Lotus in this lesson difficult, don't try to force it: continue with the bouncing action of the knees until you are supple enough. It will also help to practise the Butterfly which is shown in lesson 2 of this course, and is ideal as preparation for this pose.

Once you can get into the Half Lotus, you'll need several weeks to perfect it before moving on to the Full Lotus.

ALTERNATE LEG RAISING
Strengthens the spine, particularly the lower back and neck muscles, improves co-ordination

Lie on your back with your arms relaxed by your sides. Slowly raise your right leg to a vertical position. Raise your left leg and lower your right leg to a few inches above the floor. Raise your right leg and at the same time lower your left leg to a few inches above the floor. Continue to lower and raise each leg alternately and slowly, without touching the floor.
Repeat nine times.

THE RELAXATION POSE
Lie on your back with your feet slightly apart, your arms at your sides with your palms facing up, your head and neck relaxed. Close your eyes. Put your tongue behind your lower teeth and relax your jaw. Feel all the little muscles in your cheeks relax. As always, breathe only through your nose. Relax your mind as well as your body. Remain like this for several minutes both before and after your yoga sessions.

THE SNIFFING BREATH
Increases lung capacity, improves breathing, stimulates the respiratory mechanism

Sit in any comfortable posture, making sure your back and neck are straight. Close your right nostril with your right forefinger and exhale as deeply as possible. Pause with the breath out for a few seconds, then inhale by taking very short gentle sniffs. Do not strain. Exhale slowly and relax the chest. Repeat twice.
Repeat three times with your left nostril closed by your left forefinger.

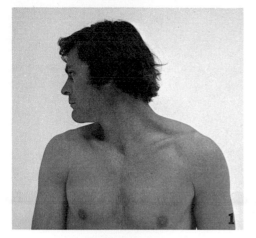

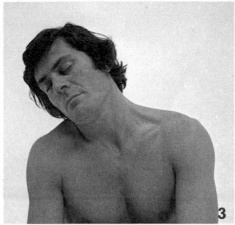

NECK EXERCISES
Releases tension in the neck muscles, in the cervical vertebrae and in the back of the shoulders

Sit in any comfortable position, making sure that the back is straight and the body relaxed. Move only your head and neck in these exercises.

1. Inhale and turn your head to the right, looking as far back as possible. Exhale and turn your head to face the front. Inhale and turn your head to the left and look back as far as possible. Exhale and face the front again.
Repeat twice to each side.

2. Then inhale and let your head drop back. Exhale, lift your head and let it fall forward. Feel the stretch at the back of the neck.

3. Inhale and roll your head round to the right as slowly as possible, letting it move with its own weight to the back. Exhale and let it roll to the left and back to the front. Repeat the head circling once in this direction and twice in the other direction.

4. Massage the back of your neck with your fingertips, making little circular movements. Try to work on the areas of tension.

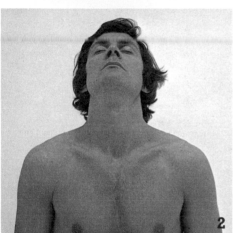

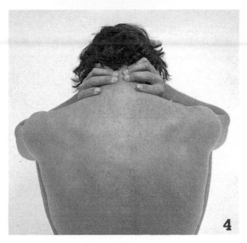

THE SIDEWAYS BEND
Stretches and slims the waist, hips and thighs

1. Kneel and stretch your right leg out sideways, and raise your arms above your head with your fingers linked. Inhale.

2. Exhale and bend sideways towards the leg. Keep your body facing the front and let the weight of your arms pull you further down. Try to relax to enable you to stretch further. Inhale and come up again.
Repeat to your left side.
Repeat twice each side.

THE STANDING TWIST
Releases tension in the whole spine, increases suppleness

Stand erect with your feet slightly apart and your body relaxed. Raise arms to shoulder height. Keeping your spine upright and your feet straight, twist the whole body round to the left whilst inhaling. Look back as far as possible. Then exhale and turn back again.

Smoothly continue to twist the whole body round to the right and inhale. Turn your head, exhale and turn back.

Repeat twice to each side.

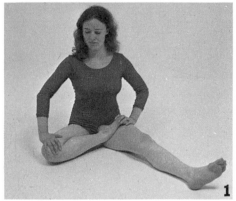

1

2

THE HALF LOTUS
This is one of the seated postures which is used for meditation, and is an essential preparation for the Full Lotus

1. To prepare for this posture stretch out the left leg and bring the right foot up onto the top of the left thigh with the heel touching the body. Bounce the right knee up and down gently. Then change legs and repeat with the left foot on top. When you can put both knees on the floor with no discomfort you can practise the Half Lotus.

2. Bend your left knee so that the heel is on the floor against your groin. Then bend your right knee, lift your right leg gently and place your foot on top of the left thigh with the sole upwards. Both knees should touch the floor. Stay in this position for a minute or two.

Repeat on the other side, with your right foot against your groin and your left foot on your right thigh.

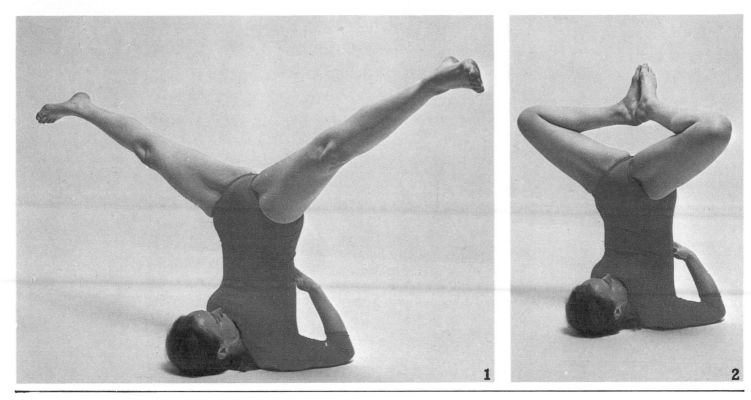

1

2

1

2

THE SHOULDERSTAND—6
In addition to the usual benefits of the Shoulderstand, this exercise stretches the inner thighs and improves circulation in the legs

Rise up into the Full Shoulderstand (see lesson nine). Hold the posture for three minutes, breathing abdominally.
1. Inhale and open your legs to form a wide 'V' shape.
2. Exhale and bring the soles of your feet together, pressing your knees out as far as possible.
Repeat the leg movement three times.
Then come down slowly from the Shoulderstand.

THE FISH—2
Stretches the thighs, strengthens the back, increases the flow of blood to the head

1. Sit on your heels in the Thunderbolt position and lean back, supporting yourself first on one and then on the other elbow. Arch your back.
2. Bend your head back, at the same time shifting the elbows forward until the crown of your head rests on the floor. Stretch your arms and put your hands on your thighs. Take three to five deep breaths.
To return, bring your elbows back to the floor and transfer your weight onto your elbows and forearms, at the same time raising your head. Sit up in the Thunderbolt posture and relax for a few seconds with closed eyes.

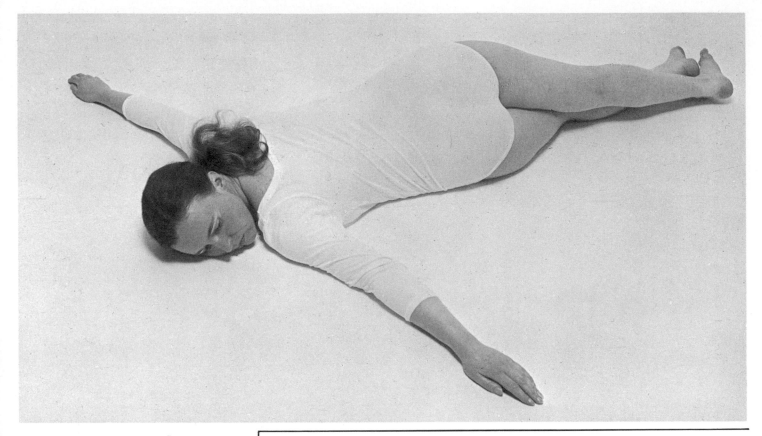

THE CROCODILE—10
Gives a corkscrew twist to the spine, stimulates and massages the internal organs

Lie on your abdomen with your chin on the floor and your arms stretched out at shoulder height. Place your right foot on top of your left foot, the heel between the big toe and second toe. Inhale. Twist your hips and legs to the left, at the same time turning your head to the left in the direction of the heels. Then twist your hips and legs to the right and at the same time turn your head to the right.
Repeat once to each side, then lie on the abdomen and exhale.
Repeat the whole exercise with the left foot on top of the right foot.

THE CHAIR
Very strengthening for the legs, particularly the muscles around the knees ; improves balance

Stand with your feet about a foot apart. Extend your forearms in front of the body with your hands hanging loose. Bend your knees and lower your body, keeping your back straight. Go down as slowly as possible and imagine that you are sitting in an armchair. Take five breaths when you are down, then rise up again slowly.
Repeat once.

106

1

2

3

THE DANCER'S POSE
Excellent for improving balance, stretching the thighs and strengthening the legs
Practise the first version before going on to the second

A. Stand upright and grasp your left ankle with your left hand. When you are well balanced raise your right arm straight above your head. With your left hand pull your left knee as far back as possible, keeping the heel close to the body and stretching your thigh. Hold this posture for five breaths.
Repeat holding your right ankle with your right hand and your left arm above your head.

B. Stand upright. Grasp your left ankle with your left hand and raise your right arm straight above your head. When balanced begin to lower your trunk forwards, raising your left leg as high as possible and stretching your left arm out in front. Hold this position for five breaths. Repeat with the right leg raised.

THE SNAKE
Stretches the back of the neck, the shoulders and the abdominal muscles, strengthens the arms

Place your body as for the Cobra with your hands at shoulder height and your forehead on the floor. Inhale and raise your head, shoulders and chest. Rise a little so that your navel is just off the floor. Then, with the strength of your arms and elbows, slide your body forwards until the navel is in line with your hands.

1. Straighten the arms a little and then 'hunch' the neck into the shoulders. Look up as high as possible, supporting yourself with your arms. Remain like this for a count of five.
2. Slowly 'unhunch' and come down as in the Cobra.
3. Immediately come into the Pose of the Child with forehead on the ground, kneeling with arms stretched out in front of you.

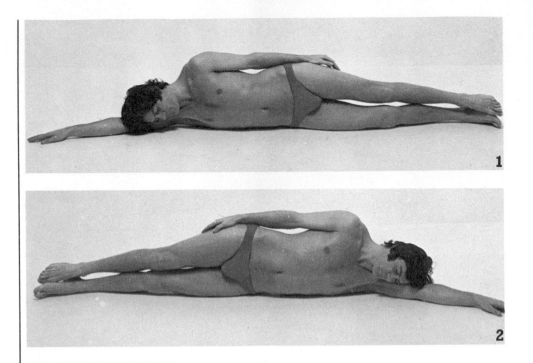

1

2

SIDE BREATHING
Improves breathing, relaxes

1. Lie on your right side with your head resting on your upper arm. Make sure that your feet are together and that you are lying straight, but relaxed. Inhale, concentrating on your left nostril, your left lung and the whole of the left side of your body. Then exhale in the same way. Repeat nine times, continuing to concentrate on the left side of your body.
2. Lie on your left side and repeat the 10 breaths, this time concentrating on your right nostril, your right lung and the whole of the right side of your body.

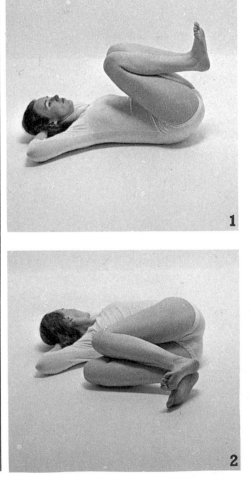

1

2

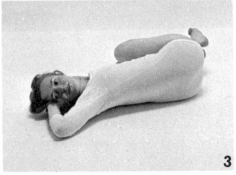

3

THE CROCODILE—11
Strengthens the muscles of the lower back and abdomen, counteracts stiffness in the neck

1. Lie on your back and link your hands behind your head. Draw your knees up to chest level, and inhale.
2. Holding the breath, slowly move your legs to the right until they touch the floor, at the same time turning your head as far as possible to the left.
3. Keeping your knees as close to your body as possible move your legs from the right to the left side of your body, at the same time turning your head to the right.
Repeat once.
Straighten your legs and bring your arms back to your sides. Then exhale and relax.

Lesson 15

When you've mastered this programme you'll be three quarters of the way towards completion of the main yoga course, and well on the road to proficiency at the physical side of yoga.

But what of the rest? The physical aspects should ideally be only the beginning. That's not to say that it can't be an end in itself: it can, like any form of exercise. But, almost inevitably, there will be other changes in your life: a greater level of tolerance, more balance and harmony, better sleep, a deeper understanding of yourself.

One of the most important of these is harmony. By practising yoga regularly you'll find that the physical harmony your body learns to express, helped by the breathing and relaxation, will lead to mental and spiritual balance. For some it happens quickly; for others it takes time. But if the application is there, so are the rewards.

THE RELAXATION POSE
Lie on your back with your feet slightly apart, your arms at your sides with your palms up, your head and neck relaxed. Close your eyes and, as always, breathe only through your nose. Concentrate on relaxing in this position before and after each yoga session.

CURLING UP—3
Strengthens the abdomen and neck muscles

1. Lie on your back with your hands clasped behind your head.
2. Slowly begin to sit up, inhaling and curling the spine, first by raising your head. Try to move up vertebrae after vertebrae.
3. Complete the inhalation when your body is straight, and look up. Start exhaling as you come down. Uncurl your spine down from the lower vertebrae first, tuck your head in and make sure that it is the last part of the body to touch the floor.
Repeat the whole exercise twice.

SHOULDER ROLLING
Relieves stiff and tense shoulders, increases flexibility of the shoulder joints

1. Sit in any comfortable posture where your back is straight and relaxed. Keeping the rest of your body still, raise your right shoulder as high as possible.
2. Slowly move your shoulder back as far as possible.
3. Continue the circular movement downwards, pulling your shoulder as far down as you can.
4. Complete the movement by bringing your shoulder forward, then finally back to the first position. Repeat this movement five times forward and six times back.
Then repeat six times in each direction with your left shoulder.

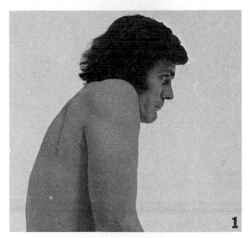

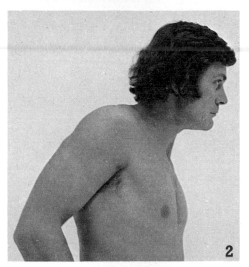

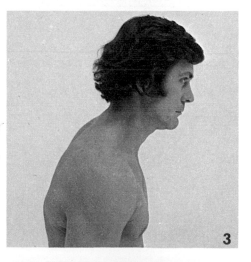

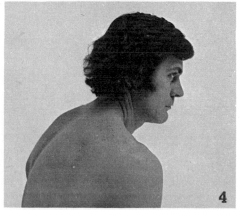

PUSHING UP
Strengthens the back, arms and thighs, slims the buttocks and thighs

1. Lie flat on your back with the palms of your hands on the floor parallel to your head and your arms and knees bent. Keep the soles of your feet flat on the floor. Inhale.
2. Hold the breath. Keeping your head on the floor press your palms firmly against the floor and raise your body. The weight now rests on your head, hands and feet. Hold for a count of five, then slowly return to the floor and exhale.

The less your knees are bent, the more difficult the exercise, so try to increase the distance between your buttocks and your feet as you practise.

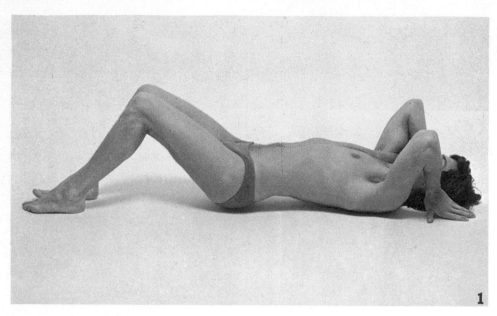

1

2

Because of the nature of the Shoulderstand exercise in this lesson, there's no illustration. For the basic Full Shoulderstand position see lesson nine.

THE SHOULDERSTAND—7
Brings a fresh supply of blood to the whole of the genital region, helping to counteract any malfunctions

Come up into the Full Shoulderstand (see lesson nine) and hold the position for three minutes, breathing abdominally. Relax your legs as much as possible. Slowly contract the anus for a few seconds, then relax again. Continue to contract and relax slowly and rhythmically for about one minute.

Slowly come down again and relax.

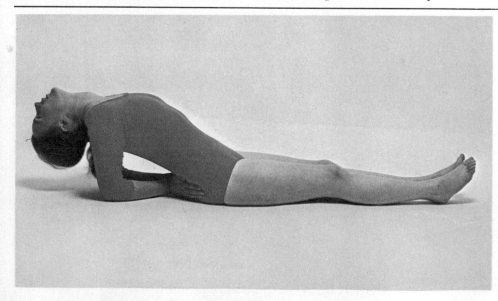

THE BREATHING FISH
This is one of the counterposes to be used after the Shoulderstand; it is excellent for expanding and developing the thorax and relaxing the neck muscles

Lie on your back and sit up, leaning on your elbows. Place the palms of your hands against your lower back with the wrists touching each other if possible. Arch your back and let your head drop back. Unlike the other version of the Fish the head does not touch the floor. Breathe consciously with the thorax, expanding your ribs sideways as you inhale; do not use the abdomen. Take 10 deep breaths. Then raise your head and relax on your back again.

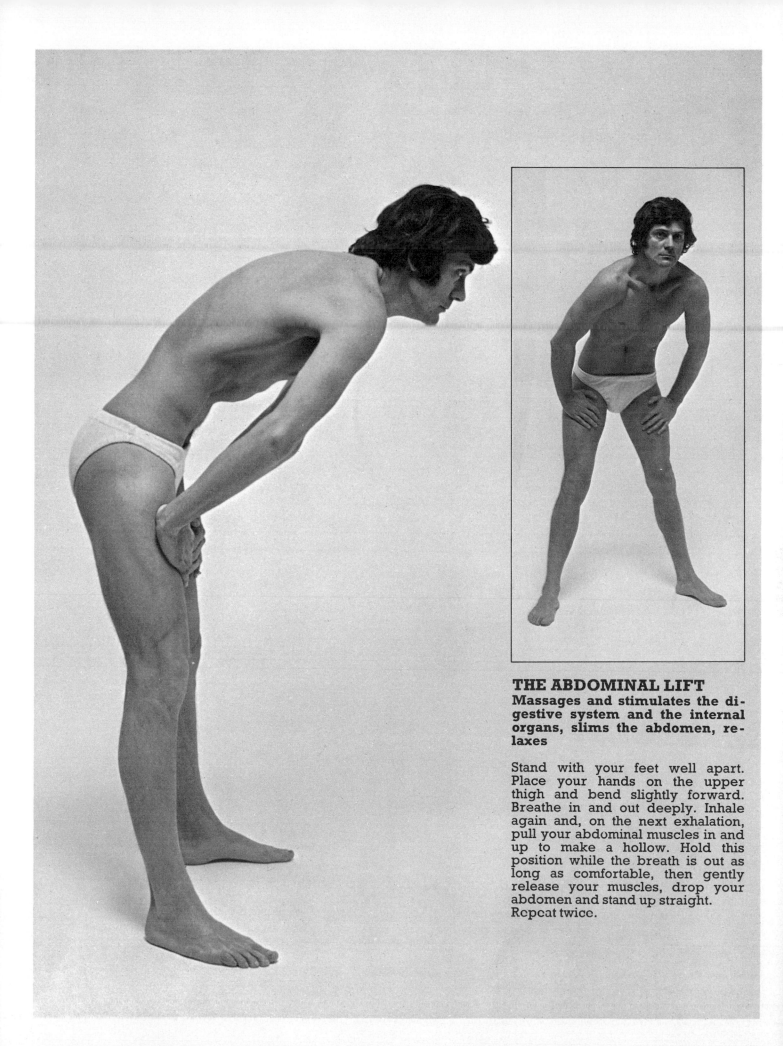

THE ABDOMINAL LIFT
Massages and stimulates the digestive system and the internal organs, slims the abdomen, relaxes

Stand with your feet well apart. Place your hands on the upper thigh and bend slightly forward. Breathe in and out deeply. Inhale again and, on the next exhalation, pull your abdominal muscles in and up to make a hollow. Hold this position while the breath is out as long as comfortable, then gently release your muscles, drop your abdomen and stand up straight. Repeat twice.

1

2

THE HALF LOCUST
This is the preparation for the Full Locust; works strongly on the lumbar region and the kidneys

1. Lie on your abdomen with your chin on the floor. Keep your feet together and your arms by your sides. Contract the muscles in the small of your back on the right side and lean on your right arm. Raise your right leg straight and in line with the body. Hold for a count of five and slowly bring it down.
2. Repeat with your left leg raised.

THE FULL LOCUST
Makes spine more supple, strengthens the arms

Lie on your abdomen with your chin on the floor. Make fists with your hands and place them under your abdomen or thighs. Inhale and exhale twice and then, on the third inhalation, swing your legs up as high as possible with a swift movement, keeping them together and straight. Hold for as long as possible, then exhale and slowly come down. Relax.
Repeat only once.

A. THE MONUMENT
Strengthens arms and legs, improves balance, makes back more supple

Lie face down with your hands as for the Cobra, in line with your shoulders. Bend your right knee and lift your left leg, resting your left knee on the sole of your right foot. When you are well balanced inhale and raise your body by straightening your arms. Bend your head and take five deep breaths. Slowly come down by bending the elbows, bringing your chest down first. Glide along the shin of your left leg with the sole and toes of your right foot. Stretch both legs on the floor. Repeat on the other side with your right leg balanced on your left foot.

B. THE TREE
Develops poise and balance, strengthens legs

Stand with your feet together. Put the sole of your left foot against the inside of your right thigh, as high as possible. Stretch your arms out sideways. Hold this posture for five breaths, then stand with eyes closed. Repeat with the right foot against your left thigh.

Lesson 16

Following this yoga course helps you to get to know better the potential and the limitations of your body. You find out where tension affects your body and how the various exercises can be used to help you to unwind.

Remember tension not only hampers you but creates a restless and disturbing aura about you to which other people respond. Relaxation is a discipline which once you have mastered it can be used to create harmony and repose about you.

Tension cannot be turned off at will as if it were a light switch. You should first find out what triggers off tension in your mind and body. Sometimes tension can be set in motion not only by emotion but by the multitude of distractions and irritations in your environment—by colour or even an object.

Colour has the power to alleviate or increase your tenseness. It can soothe or irritate depending on your personality.

An object such as a picture or an ornament can trigger off tension in much the same way. All these little things add up and if you surround yourself with needless irritants you will be distracted constantly from yourself and your goals.

It is as important then to clear the rooms in which you do your yoga of all intrusive objects or colours as it is to clear your mind of fears and anxieties. Then you can begin to relax with full consciousness instead of using half your mental energy to block out these jarring elements.

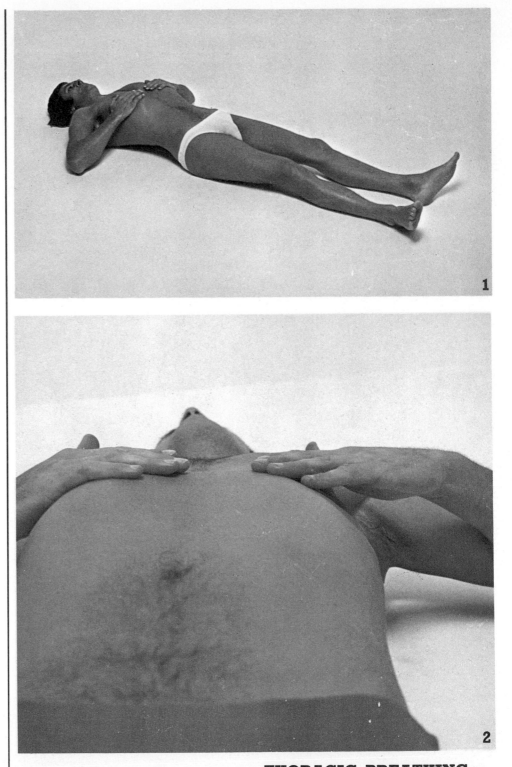

1

2

THE RELAXATION POSE
Lie on your back, feet slightly apart, arms at your sides, palms up and head and neck relaxed. Feel that all the little muscles in your cheeks relax. Imagine that a hand is slowly stroking your hair and relax your scalp. As always, breathe only through your nose. Try to relax your mind as well as your body. Do this for at least two minutes before and after each session.

THORACIC BREATHING
Increases flexibility and control of the ribcage, strengthens the muscles between the ribs

1. Take six thoracic breaths.
2. Keep your hands on your ribcage. With the next inhalation, expand only the right side of your ribcage, keeping the left side relaxed. Exhale.
3. With the next inhalation expand only the left side of your ribcage, keeping right side relaxed.
Repeat this movement of the ribcage nine times.

THE PIGEON
Stretches the back of the neck and the shoulders, acts on the spine, relieves tension

1. Kneel with your feet together and your knees apart. Put both your arms through your legs and cover the soles of your feet with your palms.
2. Keeping your buttocks down, inhale and raise your head, stretching up as far as possible.
Exhale, bring your head down again, flexing your neck the other way.
Repeat five times.

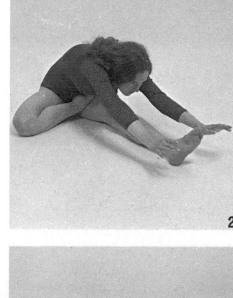

THE STICK STRETCH
Increases breath control and awareness, exercises the chest muscles, stimulates the nervous system

Lie on your back with your arms relaxed by your sides. Inhale and then exhale deeply, emptying the lungs. Without breathing, lift your arms over your head and expand the chest. Stretch with the breath held. Inhale, bringing your arms back. Exhale.
Repeat three times.

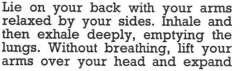

THE BACK STRETCH IN HALF LOTUS
Stretches the spine, especially the lower back, increases flexibility of the knees and thighs

Do not attempt this exercise until you can bring your knee to the floor in Half Lotus.
1. Sit with your left leg stretched out and place your right foot high on your left thigh in Half Lotus. Raise both your arms above your head and twist your trunk towards your left leg. Inhale.
2. Exhaling slowly, bend down towards your left leg, keeping your chin up and trying to stretch from your hips. Bend as low as possible. Keep your arms stretched out and try to relax, breathing normally. Inhale and return to upright position.
Repeat with your left foot on your right thigh, bending down to your right foot.

Advanced version
Practise this version only when you are able to grasp your foot from behind, still keeping your knee comfortably on the ground.
3. Sit with your right foot placed on the top of your left thigh and bring your right arm round behind your back to grasp the toes of your right foot. Raise your left arm. Inhale.
4. Bend down slowly trying to stretch from your hips. Exhale. Bend as low as possible, holding your left foot. Breathe normally and relax. Inhale and return to upright position.
Repeat once on the other side.

THE STANDING TWIST
Gives an effective twist to the small of the back, increases flexibility of the waist

Stand with your feet slightly apart and raise your arms to shoulder height. Keep your pelvis still and facing forward. Inhale while twisting from your waist upward to the left as far as possible. Exhale and turn to the front again.

Turn from your waist upward as far as possible to the right keeping your pelvis still and facing forward. Inhale as you twist. Exhale while coming back to the front.

Repeat twice more to each side.

THE SHOULDERSTAND–8
Stimulates circulation in the legs, increases flexibility of the ankles, stretches the hamstrings

Come up into the Full Shoulderstand (see Lesson 9). With your chin well tucked in take five deep abdominal breaths. Flex your ankles with your toes pointing towards your head and then relax them. Repeat this movement five times. Keeping your legs still, make five circles with both feet toward the right and five to the left. With your feet slightly apart make circles in opposite directions, first one way and then the other.

Relax your feet, breathe deeply again, and slowly come down into the Plough.

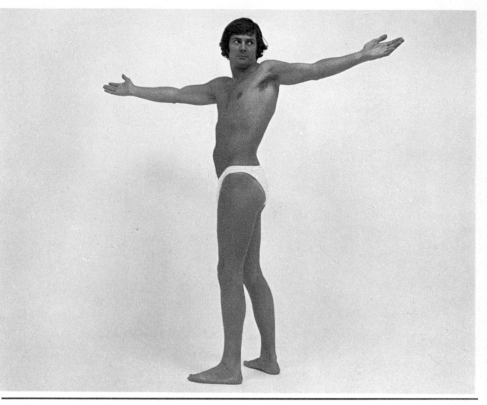

THE PLOUGH–2
Stretches the spine and strengthens the thigh muscles

1. After you have done the Shoulderstand, go straight down into the Plough (see Lesson 11). When both feet touch the floor remain with your toes on the floor and your knees straight. Take five abdominal breaths.

2. Slowly move your legs apart as far as possible, keeping your toes on the floor. Then place your arms on the floor in front of you. Hold for five breaths.

Slowly come back to first Plough position and return to the Relaxation Pose.

THE CROCODILE—12
Gives a gentle twist to the lumbar region, stretches the hips, increases suppleness of the neck

1. Lie on your front with your arms stretched out at shoulder height. Bend your knees and hold them about 18 inches apart. (When twisting, the sole of one foot should touch the knee of the other leg so the distance will vary according to the length of your legs.) Inhale.
2. Move your legs and hips towards the right until both feet touch the floor and at the same time turn your head to the right.
3. Raise your feet again and twist to the left, moving your hips at the same time until your feet touch the floor at the other side. Turn your head to the left.
Repeat five times.

THE DOLPHIN—2
Stimulates the circulation, improves the complexion and balance, relaxes

1. Use a small cushion or folded blanket for your head. Kneel and place your hands by your head to form a triangle. If you prefer, place the palms of your hands on the floor about a foot below your head. Rise up on your toes.
2. Straighten your legs and breathe deeply with your abdomen. When you are well balanced take your hands away and link them behind your back. Hold for five to ten deep breaths.
Place your hands on the floor and slowly come down.

117

THE COBRA–8
Increases suppleness of the spine, stretches the abdominal muscles

1. Place your hands in the Cobra with your elbows near your sides. Inhaling slowly, raise your head.
2. Continue rising smoothly until your chest is off the floor. Finally straighten your arms and stretch up with your head back.
3. Come down again bending your arms and letting your back once more hold your weight. Exhale. When you can, lift your hands so that you are supported by the strength of your back. Breathe normally. Hold for two breaths.
When you come down bring your forehead back to the floor giving a counterflex to the back of your neck. Relax.
Repeat once.

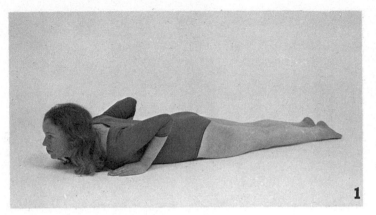

1

2

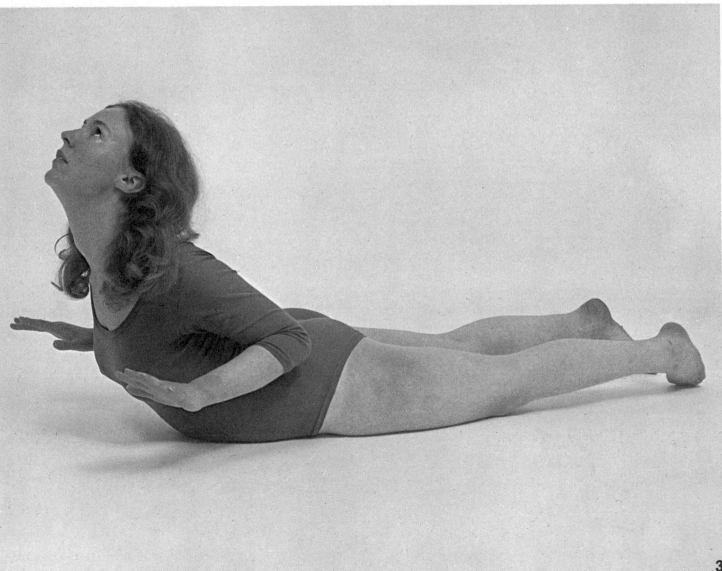

3

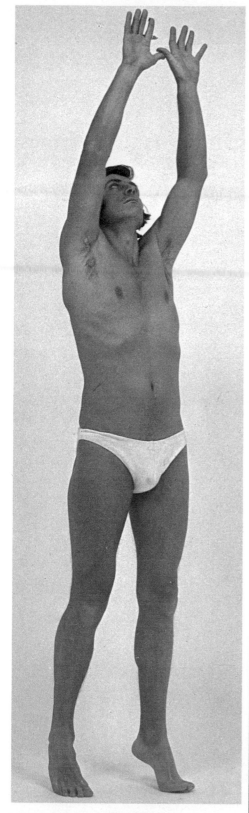

THE PALM TREE
Stretches and tones the intestines, relieves wind and constipation

Stand upright and stretch your arms above your head with your fingers splayed and thumbs linked. Rise up on your toes and look up at your hands. Breathe normally and take 10 steps forward and 10 back.
Relax your arms and legs, then repeat or

Regular, daily yoga builds up your self-confidence in many subtle ways. The deeper and more relaxed breathing you acquire helps you to overcome tension which can sometimes intrude just when you want to be collected and sure of yourself.
And the new poise you radiate is definite proof to others that you are self-assured — ready to cope with a variety of situations.
The effects of such confidence extend into most parts of your life. Whether you are talking casually, dancing, untangling a problem at work and even just sitting on your own, the benefits of yoga are apparent.

THE EAGLE
Stimulates circulation in the legs, strengthens the calf muscles, improves balance

There are two versions of the posture, the static and the dynamic. Twist your right leg around your left leg and put your right elbow under your left elbow bringing your hands together. Press both your arms and legs tightly together. your arms and legs reversed.
While in the first position, bend your left knee and slowly come down as low as possible, trying to keep your body upright. Hold for a count of five. Then rise up slowly.
Repeat on the other side with your legs reversed.

Lesson 17

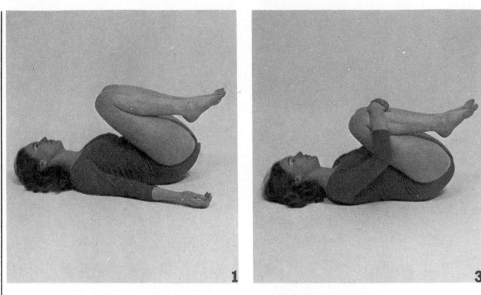

1

3

Now that you have progressed this far with the *Unisex Yoga* course, you will be capable of exercises and postures that you would have found impossible when you began. Your body has become more supple, and you are benefiting from the peace of mind that regular yoga practice gives to you.

At this stage you may feel quite satisfied with the progress you are making and you are perhaps anxious to go still further and to develop more advanced techniques. Don't be impatient. You must never force the pace with yoga training. While you learn to master new exercises don't neglect those that you now find quite simple to perform.

Never forget the relaxation pose at the beginning and end of each session. When properly practised this posture will relax not only the muscles of the body but the nervous system as well. Begin by concentrating your mind on all points of your body from the feet upwards. Consciously relax your tense muscles. Make sure that the face, forehead and neck are completely relaxed and loosen your mouth, jaw and tongue. Check to make sure that no points of tension remain.

With your body now limp and motionless your brain will begin to relax as well. Let all thoughts and impulses flow from your mind. Breathe deeply and rhythmically imagining that with each breath you are recharging your body, inhaling energy and exhaling tension. You may even find it helpful to imagine that you are on an empty beach or mountain top where your daily problems and anxieties no longer exist.

2

THE RELAXATION POSE
Lie on your back, feet slightly apart, arms at your sides, palms up and head and neck relaxed. Feel that all the little muscles in your cheeks relax. Imagine that a hand is slowly stroking your hair and relax your scalp. As always, breathe only through your nose. Try to relax your mind as well as your body. Do this for at least two minutes before and after each session.

THE STANDING BREATH
Increases awareness, improves breath control and circulation

Stand with your feet about 14 inches apart, your arms hanging loosely at your sides and your whole body completely relaxed. Close your eyes. Inhale abdominally and raise your arms above your head.
Exhale slowly through your mouth, bending downward and letting your relaxed body hang down from the waist (see Lesson seven). Continue exhaling through your mouth until as much air as possible is squeezed out of your lungs. Pause in this position for a few seconds without inhaling.
Raise your arms and body, inhaling at the same time.
Repeat three times.

THE BACK STRENGTHENER
Strengthens the back and lumbar region, helps counteract a hollow spine, relieves pain

1. Lie on your back with arms relaxed by your sides. Bring both knees up to your chest.
2. Inhale and raise your head level with your knees, while keeping your back pressed to the floor. Straighten your legs and hold them above the floor without arching your back. Exhale.
3. Relax by bringing your knees back to your chest. Clasp them and put your head back on the floor. Breathe deeply from the abdomen until your breath is normal again.
Repeat twice.
Try to increase the holding time and to lower your legs nearer to the floor during further practice.

ARM TURNING
Loosens the shoulders, counter-acts stiffness and relieves tension

1. Stand with your feet slightly apart and raise both arms to waist level. Inhale keeping your arms straight and turn both arms as far outwards as possible.
2. Exhale and turn your arms inwards.
Repeat three times.
A second version of this exercise can be performed with both arms at shoulder height.

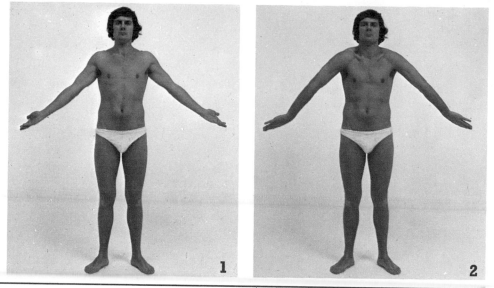

1

2

1

2

THE SCALES
Strengthens abdominal muscles and back, improves balance and co-ordination, stretches the hamstrings, neck and shoulders

1. Lie on your back and slowly raise your head and arms a few inches keeping them both straight. Breathe normally. Rise up further, stretching your hands towards your toes.
2. Clasp your toes. Keep your legs as straight as possible. Hold this posture for five breaths.
Slowly release and come down in the same way.
Repeat once.

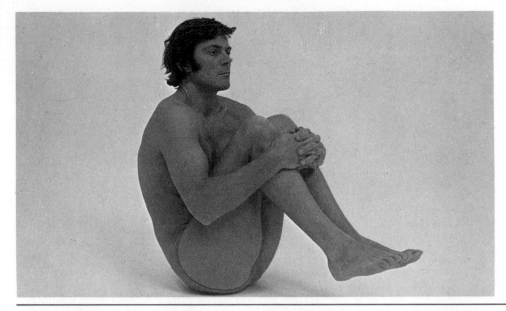

THE BALANCING SEAT
Relaxes, improves balance

Sit with your legs drawn up and clasp your hands around your knees. Lean backwards and lift your feet a few inches off the floor balancing on your buttocks. Breathe calmly. If you like, rest your forehead on your knees.

This posture can be practised at any time and comfortably held for long periods.

THE SIDEWAYS TURN
Stretches the thighs and hips, increases flexibility of the waist and back, improves co-ordination

1. Place your left knee on the floor a few inches behind your right foot and bend your right knee. Stretch out your arms at shoulder height. Transfer your body weight forwards to your right leg keeping your spine upright.
2. Inhale. Twist your body from the waist to the left looking as far left as possible and using your arms for balance.
Exhale and come back to the centre. Turn to the right as far as possible. Repeat twice on both sides.
Alternate the exercise with right knee on the floor and left foot forward.

1

2

THE SHOULDERSTAND—9
Increases flexibility of the thighs, stretches the tendons, strengthens the neck and shoulders

Go up into the Full Shoulderstand (see Lesson nine). Hold for three minutes. Breathe deeply with your abdomen and keep your chin well tucked in.
Stretch your right leg forwards and your left leg backwards as far as possible.
Slowly move your right leg backwards and your left leg forwards as far as possible.
Slowly continue this 'scissor' movement. Try to stretch further each time. Breathe normally and move your legs five times each way.
Return to the Full Shoulderstand.
Slowly bring your legs down into the Plough posture.

THE PLOUGH—3
Stretches the spine, loosens shoulders and neck muscles

Move into the Full Plough position (see Lesson seven). Stretch your arms out behind your head keeping your toes on the ground. Hold for five deep breaths. Support your back once more and slowly lower your body to the floor.

THE MOVING CAT
Strengthens the arms, neck, shoulders and spine, tones up the abdomen, improves breath control, increases flexibility

1. Kneel, place your forehead on the floor and stretch your arms forward, elbows straight and palms flat on the floor. Make sure that there is enough space for your body to move between your hands during the exercise.
2. Move your trunk forwards keeping your chin about an inch above the floor. Inhale.
3. As you continue to move forwards raise the elbows and support more of your body weight with your arms.
4. Still keeping low above the ground, move further forwards and straighten your body. Lower your body from the navel downwards to the floor. Come up into the Cobra. Complete the inhalation.
5. Straighten your arms and tuck your chin into your chest.
6. Exhale while arching your back, moving your trunk backwards.
7. Slowly lower your buttocks and continue exhaling.
Return to starting position.
Repeat this exercise twice, moving as slowly and smoothly as possible while co-ordinating your breathing with the movement.

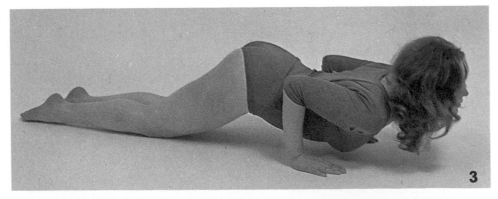

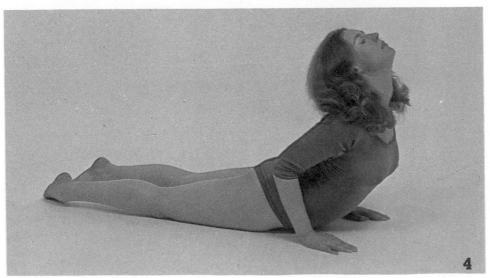

Regular yoga practice benefits both your body and mind. When you perform the exercises you have to concentrate on several things at the same time. It is important that you are always aware of what your body is doing and that you do not repeat the exercises mechanically. By learning to be aware of your body you will become more aware of yourself and what goes on around you. You will also become more aware of other people. This, in turn, will help you increase the quality of your entire life.

5

THE MONKEY WALK
Stretches the hamstrings, strengthens the legs, tones hip muscles, back and shoulders

Stand with the palms of your hands and soles of your feet flat on the floor with elbows and knees straight. Keep them straight throughout.
Walk by moving your left arm and leg forwards simultaneously and alternately with your right arm and leg.
Take ten steps forwards and ten steps backwards.

6

7

THE WINDMILL
Stretches and slims waist, massages internal organs, relieves constipation

Stand with your feet about three feet apart and link your hands above your head with your arms straight (see Lesson eight). Twist your trunk to the left. While exhaling, slowly make a half circle down to the left and then to the centre front with arms straight. Continue the circle smoothly and begin inhaling while you move to the right. Move upwards with trunk and arms until you are standing upright and facing forwards.
Repeat twice.
Perform this exercise in the other direction three times.

Lesson 18

Unlike most philosophies, yoga cannot be understood simply by reading books about it. It has to be experienced. But there is one particular word which everybody who is sincerely interested in yoga ought to know. This is the word 'equanimity'. It means evenness of temper, a state of inner tranquillity and the ability to accept what comes. It should become the objective of everyone who practises yoga. Indeed, without achieving a degree of equanimity yoga practice is meaningless.

The meditative postures which are part of the *Unisex Yoga* course will help you to achieve this calmness of mind. In this lesson we describe the 'comfortable posture', one of the easier meditation postures. While sitting in this way you may find it helpful to focus your attention on some small object placed in front of you. Concentrate on the colour and shape of the object and try to stop your mind from wandering off at a tangent. When your eyes begin to water, close them and make an effort to keep the image in your mind's eye.

You will find that this exercise will increase your powers of concentration and make you more efficient in your domestic and working life. It will also help you to achieve equanimity.

THE RELAXATION POSE

Lie on your back with your feet slightly apart, your arms at your sides and your palms up, your head and neck relaxed. Close your eyes and, as always, breathe only through your nose. Concentrate on relaxing in this position for several minutes before and after each yoga session.

THE WARMING BREATH

Relaxes the body, aids digestion, counteracts insomnia

Lie on your back with your legs bent, knees touching and soles of your feet flat on the floor. Place your hands on either side of your ribcage on your solar plexus. Concentrate on the area contained between your hands and spine. As you inhale imagine you are drawing air from the back of your spine up to your hands. As you exhale imagine that the air flows from your hands and back through your body to the floor. Within a few minutes you will begin to feel a warmth within your body. Concentrate on this warm sensation and feel your body relaxing from within.
Breathe in this way for five minutes.

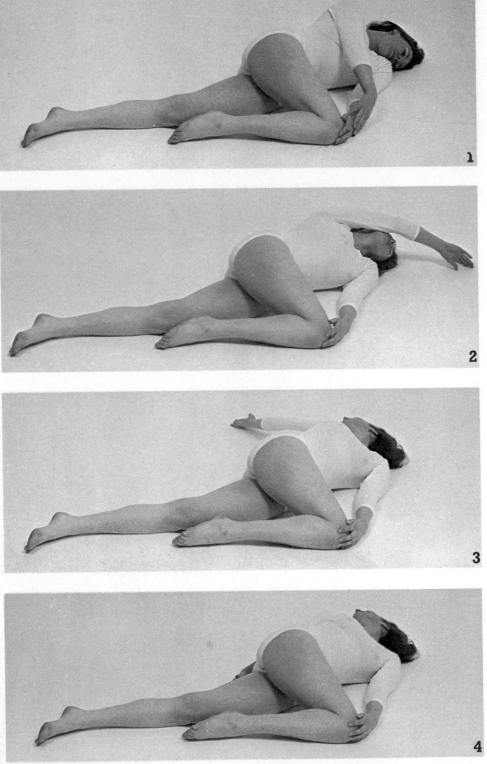

THE MOON

Loosens stiff shoulders, stretches the hips and neck

1. Lie on your back. Twist your body to the left, bend your right knee and place your right leg and knee on the floor. Put the palm of your left hand on your right knee and your right palm on top of your left hand.
2. Move your arm as if you were beginning to draw a circle on the floor. Continue to move your arm smoothly in a circle watching your hand all the time.
3. Bring your arm behind your head keeping your fingers on the floor. Continue the circle round to the right, still following your hand with your eyes.
4. Bring your arm slowly round and down towards your left leg. Finally, bring your right hand down to touch your left thigh.
Circle back again in the same way. Repeat twice. Change sides and repeat three circles forwards and backwards with your left arm.

THE STANDING TWIST
Exercises and reduces tension in the whole spine, increases flexibility of the waist and shoulders

Stand with your feet slightly apart and your body relaxed. Raise your arms to shoulder height (see Lesson sixteen). Keep your spine upright and your hips still and facing forwards. Inhale while twisting your trunk as far as possible to the left. Exhale and return to the front again. Inhale while twisting your trunk to the right in the same way. Exhale and return to the front.
Repeat twice to each side.

THE COMFORTABLE POSTURE
A meditative posture which is particularly comfortable if you cannot do the Half Lotus

Sit with your right knee bent and your right heel tucked into your groin. Bend your left knee and place your left leg on the floor outside your right leg. Make sure that your back and head are straight. Place your hands on your knees. Sit quietly for a while.
Repeat with your right leg outside your left leg.

127

1

2

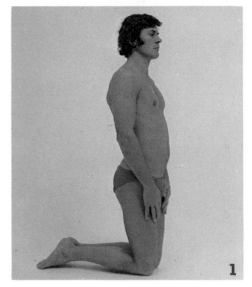

THE KNEELING EXERCISE
Strengthens the thigh muscles, improves concentration and muscular control

1. Kneel straight with your palms on your thighs.
2. Lean back slowly keeping your back and head in a straight line. Go back as far as possible using your leg muscles to support your weight. Slowly come up in the same way. Repeat twice, moving as slowly as possible in order to derive the greatest benefit.

1

THE COW
Straightens the spine, loosens the shoulders

1. Bend your left knee and place your heel against your right buttock. Bend your right knee and bring it over your left knee. Remain in this position for five breaths.
2. Bend your right elbow and put your hand down the centre of your back. Bend your left elbow and put your left hand up the back until your hands meet. Link your fingers. Keep your spine and head erect. Remain in this posture for five deep breaths.
3. Repeat with your left leg bent over your right and your left arm upwards.

THE SHOULDERSTAND—10
Stretches the thighs, improves balance, increases circulation in the legs

Come up into the Full Shoulderstand (see Lesson Nine). Remain in this position and take five deep abdominal breaths.

Inhale. Slowly bend your left knee while keeping your right leg straight. Exhale and bring the left knee as low as possible without moving your right leg. Inhale. Raise your left knee.

Repeat with right leg, exhaling as you bring down your knee, inhaling as you bring it up.

Repeat with each leg.

Slowly come down from the Full Shoulderstand.

2

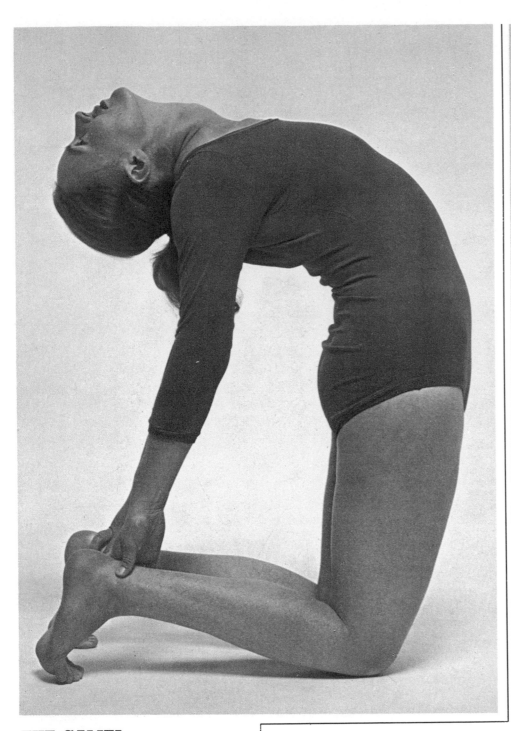

THE CAMEL
Massages the kidneys and adrenal glands, speeds the metabolism, flexes the spine, stretches the shoulders and thighs

Kneel with your toes on the floor and your head and spine straight. Bend backwards from your waist. Reach back with your hands to touch your ankles. Drop your head backwards and remain in this posture, breathing deeply for five breaths. To come back, lower your buttocks slowly while raising your head and shoulders until you are sitting on your heels.
Repeat once.
Do not practise this exercise until your neck and spine are sufficiently flexible.

THE FLYING POSE
Stretches the limbs, strengthens the small of the back, thigh and shoulder muscles

1. Lie on your abdomen with your arms at right angles to your body and your chin on the floor. Inhale and stretch your arms outwards, keeping them on the floor. Exhale and relax.
Repeat three times.
2. Inhale. Stretch and raise your arms, legs and head a few inches above the floor so that your body is balanced on the abdomen. Exhale and come down slowly.
Repeat three times.

THE RAISED BOW
Reduces tension in the back muscles, increases concentration and body control

Position yourself on all fours (see Lesson thirteen). Place your left forearm on the floor in line with your shoulders, your palm down flat. Position your right knee carefully because your weight will be distributed between your right leg and your left arm. Grasp your left ankle with your right hand, then raise your left leg as high as possible, and look up. Hold for a count of five, then slowly come back to the starting position.
Repeat with your right arm on the floor and your left hand clasping your right leg.

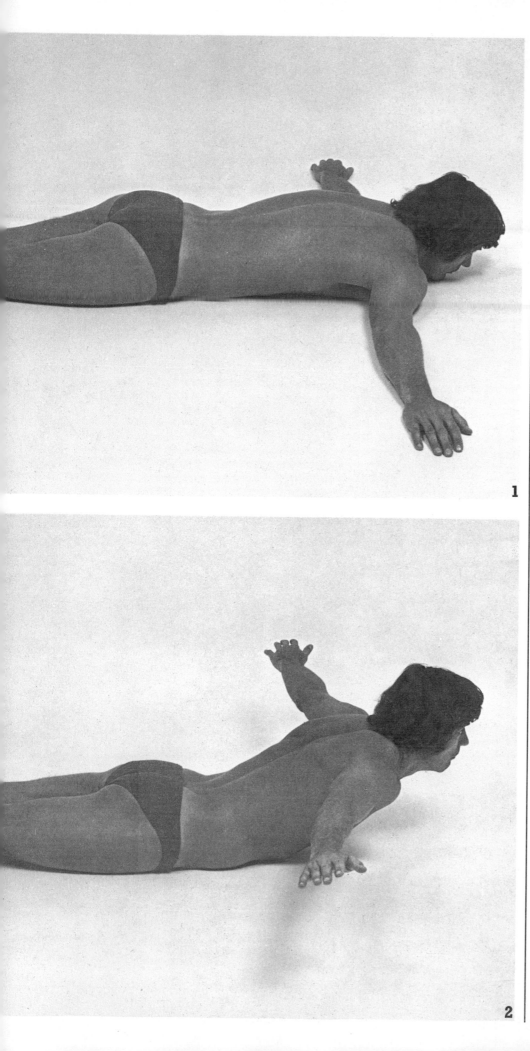

1

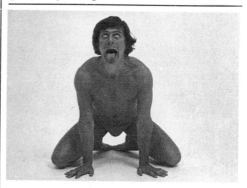

THE LION
Stretches the tongue and jaw, tones up the facial muscles, improves the complexion, helps to cure sore throats

Kneel with the knees apart. Lean forward and partially support your weight on your finger tips. Open your mouth, stick out your tongue as far as possible so that it touches the chin and turn your eyeballs upwards to stretch your eye muscles. Breathe normally through the nose. Hold for five breaths. Relax your face and close your eyes.
Repeat twice.

THE TRIANGLE—5
Loosens the spine, massages the abdominal muscles

Stand with your feet well apart and link your hands behind your back (see Lesson nine). Turn your right foot outwards and bend your right leg. Inhale. As you exhale, bend forwards and touch your right knee with your forehead. Relax in this position for a count of five, then inhale and straighten up.
Repeat with your left leg.
If you find this easy, then bend your right leg further and try to ease your head down as near to your foot as possible. Relax for a count of five, inhale and straighten up.
Repeat with your left leg.

2

131

Lesson 19

Now that you have progressed this far with this unique yoga course you will have noticed many changes in your mind and body. The increase in your self-confidence will be noticeable not only to yourself but also to your friends. Your personality will have grown stronger and you will be happier in your personal and business relationships.

At this point we introduce the Full Lotus posture. This is one of the most beautiful of the yoga postures and, once mastered, one of the most relaxing. The Full Lotus is not the final goal of yoga practice—as it is sometimes thought—but it is an excellent posture for prolonged meditation. It is also incorporated in some of the exercises that are featured in the next lesson.

If you are a beginner do not practise the Full Lotus after a hot bath—you might tear a ligament. And don't force your body into the posture—you will be able to do it in the future if you continue with your regular practice.

For meditation it is most important to choose a position in which you feel comfortable. With continued practice you will begin to grow 'an extra skin' which protects you from negative influences and makes you less vulnerable to the pressures and problems of your daily life.

1

THE RELAXATION POSE
Lie on your back with your feet slightly apart, your arms at your sides and your palms up, your head and neck relaxed. Close your eyes and, as always, breathe only through your nose. Concentrate on relaxing in this position for several minutes before and after each yoga session.

DEEP BREATHING
Relaxes, calms, increases lung capacity and breath control.

Lie on your back with your arms relaxed by your sides. Concentrate on your abdomen, particularly on the region of the navel. Inhale, filling your abdomen so that it rises. Exhale, feeling your abdomen sink. Repeat five times.
Now concentrate on your ribcage. Inhale, expanding your ribs sideways. Exhale, relaxing your ribcage. Do not move your abdomen during this exercise.
Repeat five times.
Take five more abdominal breaths and five thoracic breaths, feeling their contrasting physical effects.

2

THE CIRCLE
Stretches the hips, tones up the spine and small of the back

1. Lie on your back with your legs apart and your arms stretched out behind your head.
2. Begin to circle your body to the right, keeping your hands on the floor and your head and trunk as low as possible. Do not move your legs and keep your body as relaxed as possible throughout the exercise.
3. Continue to circle smoothly until your hands are centred between your legs. Lean forwards and remain relaxed.
4. Continue circling your body, extending your arms as far as possible, until you come back to your starting position.
Repeat twice.
Circle three times in the opposite direction.

3

THE DOG
Exercises the tongue, stimulates the jaw and facial muscles, helps to alleviate sore throats

Kneel with your knees about two feet apart. Lean forwards and place your hands on the floor with your wrists together and fingers pointing backwards. Open your mouth and stretch your tongue out so that it touches your chin. Inhale through your nose, exhale through your mouth, at the same time moving your tongue to the right. Inhale through your nose and move your tongue across to the left. Exhale through your mouth.
Continue slowly moving your tongue from side to side ten times, inhaling through your nose and exhaling through your mouth.

4

THE FULL LOTUS
A position used for deep meditation in which the body is held upright and balanced

Place your right foot against the left side of your groin with the sole turned up (see Lesson 14). Bend your left leg and gently lift the ankle, placing your foot against the right side of the groin. Place your hands on your knees with your palms upwards or downwards so that your first finger touches the joint of your thumb and your other fingers are straight.

Repeat with your right leg on top. Be careful not to strain your knees when practising this posture. Always repeat on both sides.

THE SHOULDER BOW
Stretches the spine, particularly the upper vertebrae, tones up the thighs and hips

Lie on your back, bend your knees and grasp your ankles with your hands. Inhale while slowly raising your body. Keep your head straight so that your chin is tucked into your chest. Exhale, and come down again.

Repeat five times.

If you find the exercise too difficult to perform leave your hands on the floor without holding your ankles.

1

THE SHOULDERSTAND—11
Stretches and strengthens the spine, thighs and hips, slims the abdomen, loosens pelvic joints

Come up into the Full Shoulderstand (see Lesson nine).

THE CUCKOO
Strengthens the arms, improves balance

Kneel with your toes on the floor and your hands palms downwards in front of your knees. Bend your elbows slightly and lean forwards placing your knees just above your elbows. Bend your elbows a little more, lean forwards and raise your feet from the floor, keeping them together. Hold this pose for five slow deep breaths. Bring your feet down again and then relax in the kneeling posture.

1. Bend your left knee backwards and your right knee forwards.
2. Slowly lower your left leg towards the floor while arching your back and supporting it with both hands at the base of the ribcage.
3. Lower your right leg until the toes of both your feet are on the floor.
4. Lower your heels to the floor and remain in this posture keeping the pelvis well up. Take five deep abdominal breaths.
Kick up with your left leg to come back into the Full Shoulderstand. Come down again, this time landing with your right leg.
This exercise should only be attempted when the back is strong and flexible. It should be performed slowly and with control.

THE BOW
Improves posture, massages the abdomen, strengthens the spine

Lie face down with your arms at your sides and your chin on the floor. Bend your legs and, keeping your knees slightly apart, hold your ankles or feet. The big toes should be touching. Keeping your arms straight and your toes together, raise your legs and then raise your head. Allow your feet to pull your arms up higher, so that your chest also leaves the floor. Bend your head back. Your feet should always be higher than your head. Hold for a count of six.
This exercise should only be attempted after you have been practising yoga for several months.

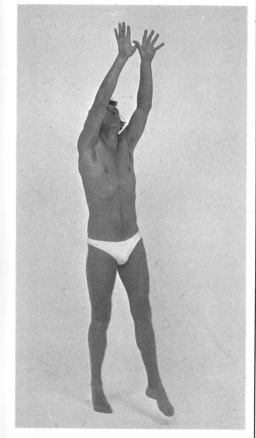

THE PALM TREE
Stretches the body, massages the digestive organs, strengthens legs and shoulders

Stand with your feet a few inches apart and raise your arms above your head with your thumbs linked and fingers spread wide apart. Rise up on your toes and look up at your hands. Take one step forward with your left foot, keeping your knee straight. Take one step forward with your right foot, keeping your knee straight. Walk for twenty steps in this way, looking up at the hands all the time. Lower your arms and heels and relax.
Repeat once.

THE TRIANGLE—6
Stretches the hips and hamstrings, loosens the body

1. Stand with your feet about three feet apart and stretch out your arms at shoulder level. Inhale. Exhale and twist your body from the waist downwards towards the right. Place the palm of your left hand in front of your right foot and look up at your right hand. Inhale, and come up again. Repeat on the other side.

2. Inhale with your arms stretched out at shoulder level. Exhale and twist your body from your waist downwards towards the right. This time place your left palm behind your right foot and look up at your right hand. Inhale, and come up again. Repeat on the other side.

3. Inhale with your arms stretched out at shoulder level. Exhale, twisting your body in the other direction so that your face is to the front and you come down to the right. Place your right palm in front of your right foot and look up at your left hand. Inhale and come up again.
Repeat on the other side.
Repeat the exercise once, bending to the left

THE ONE-LEG POSE
Strengthens the knees, expands the chest, improves balance

Stand straight and place one ankle just above your knee. Inhale, raise both arms and place your palms together above your head. Exhale and slowly bend your straight leg. Lower yourself as far as possible keeping your trunk upright. Hold for a count of five. Rise and inhale. Repeat once.
Repeat twice on the other leg

Lesson 20

Now that you have come to the end of this yoga course, it does not mean that you have finished with yoga. It should become an integral part of your life, and regular practice brings you cumulative benefits.

You should continue to practise daily, perfecting the postures and movements that you have already learned and going back to some of those that you might have neglected.

If you have missed out the Sun Worship exercises or the Yogic Breathing, for example, take this opportunity to master them. And if there were some exercises that you found particularly satisfying in the earlier lessons, you can now devote more time to them. Pick out a variety of your favourite exercises and practise them until you know them well enough to perform them without having to read the instructions.

Yoga can be practised by people of both sexes and all ages. The rewards that you reap from regular practice include increased physical fitness, greater mental awareness, tranquility of mind and renewed energy.

You should try to practise yoga daily, but you should not think of it as a duty. Above all, yoga should give you satisfaction and pleasure.

THE RELAXATION POSE
Lie on your back, feet slightly apart, arms at your sides, palms up and head and neck relaxed. Feel that all the little muscles in your cheeks relax. Imagine that a hand is slowly stroking your hair and relax your scalp. As always, breathe only through your nose. Try to relax your mind as well as your body. Do this for at least two minutes before and after each session.

BREATHING
Relaxes and calms

Sit in the Thunderbolt (see Lesson four) or in any posture where your back is straight and relaxed. Close your eyes and concentrate on your breathing, particularly your exhalation. Focus your mind on your breath passing out of your nostrils to about two inches beyond your nose. Breathe in this way for at least three minutes.

THE PANTHER STRETCH
Releases tension, counteracts stiffness in the arms, shoulders back and hips

Sit on your heels with your knees wide apart and bend forwards, keeping your buttocks on your heels. Place your hands on the floor in front of you. Bend the fingers of your right hand, tensing your hand. Stretch your arm as far forwards as possible and crook your fingers onto the floor. Claw backwards towards your body like a cat scratching with its paw.
Repeat the clawing movement with your left hand.
Claw five times with each hand. Inhale and sit up, bringing your knees together and relaxing in the Thunderbolt.

THE KNEE SUPPORT POSTURE
Strengthens the feet, legs and lumbar region, improves balance

Squat on your toes with your feet a few inches apart. Link your hands in front of you and straighten your back so that your head and spine are in a straight line. Remain balanced in this posture for ten breaths.

THE ARCHER
Loosens the knees and ankles, increases flexibility of the pelvic joints, strengthens the arms

1. Sit with your left leg stretched forwards. Bend your right leg and hold your right ankle with your right hand and your toes with your left hand. Bring your toes up to your forehead.
2. Still holding your toes up to your forehead, stretch your right arm forwards over your right leg and grasp the toes of your left foot. Remain in this position for five deep slow breaths.
Repeat with your right leg stretched forwards, your left leg bent and your left ankle in your left hand. Hold for five breaths.

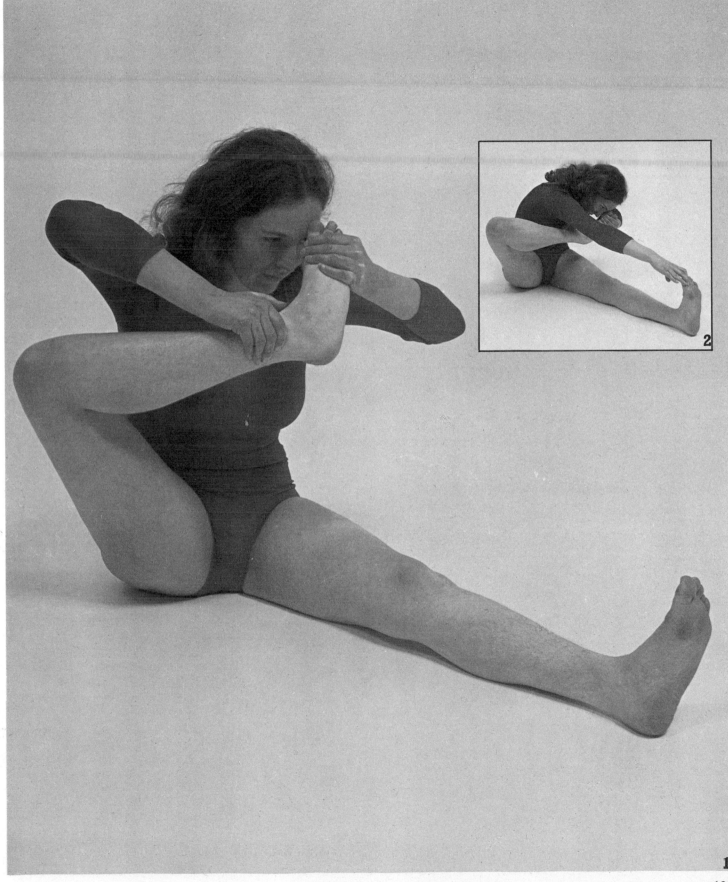

2

1

1

2

THE SIDE STAND
Strengthens the arms and legs, tones up all the body muscles, improves balance

1. Lie on your right side with your legs together, your left hand on your left thigh and your body straight. Bend your right elbow and place the palm of your right hand under your right shoulder with your fingers spread out.

2. Press down with your right hand and raise your body by straightening your right arm. Remain balanced like this for a count of five. Bend your arm and come down. Repeat on the opposite side.

THE RAISED LOTUS
Strengthens the arms, thighs and lumbar region

Sit in the Lotus posture and place your palms on either side of your thighs with your fingers spread out. Inhale, pressing down on your hands and raising your body as high as possible so that your weight is supported by your hands. Remain like this for three breaths. Repeat with opposite legs crossed.

THE SHOULDERSTAND—12
Strengthens the spine, stretches the leg muscles and tendons, tones up the hips and thighs

Come up into the Full Shoulderstand. Come down slowly into the Bridge by lowering first your right then your left leg (see Lesson nineteen). Remain in the Bridge with both feet flat on the floor for three breaths.

Inhale and raise your right leg as high as possible. Exhale and bring it down again. Inhale and raise your left leg as high as possible. Exhale and bring it down again. Repeat raising each leg twice more. Come up into the Shoulderstand again and slowly come down into the Plough.

THE PLOUGH—4
Flexes the spine in the opposite direction to the previous exercise, stretches the legs, strengthens thighs and hips

From the Shoulderstand come down into the Plough (see Lesson seven). Stretch your arms out behind your back. Inhale and spread your legs as wide apart as possible keeping your toes on the floor. Exhale and bring them back together again, still keeping your toes on the floor. Repeat five times.

Slowly come down from the Plough.

141

FISH IN LOTUS

Stretches the thighs, flexes the spine and pelvis, stimulates the kidneys and adrenal glands

1. Sit in the Lotus with your arms behind your body, your palms flat on the floor and your fingers pointing forwards.

2. Lean back and rest on your elbows and forearms. Arch your back, shift your elbows forward and drop your head until the crown rests on the floor.

3. With your body weight supported by your head bring your arms up and hold your toes. Take five slow deep breaths.
Bring body upright by resting your weight on your elbows and forearms and slowly raising your head up into the sitting position.

4. A second version of this exercise can be performed with the hands held as in prayer.

5. A third version can be performed by stretching your arms out behind your head. Return by straightening your legs out of the Lotus posture and relaxing on your back.
The first version of this exercise can be carried out in water; you will find that your body will float.

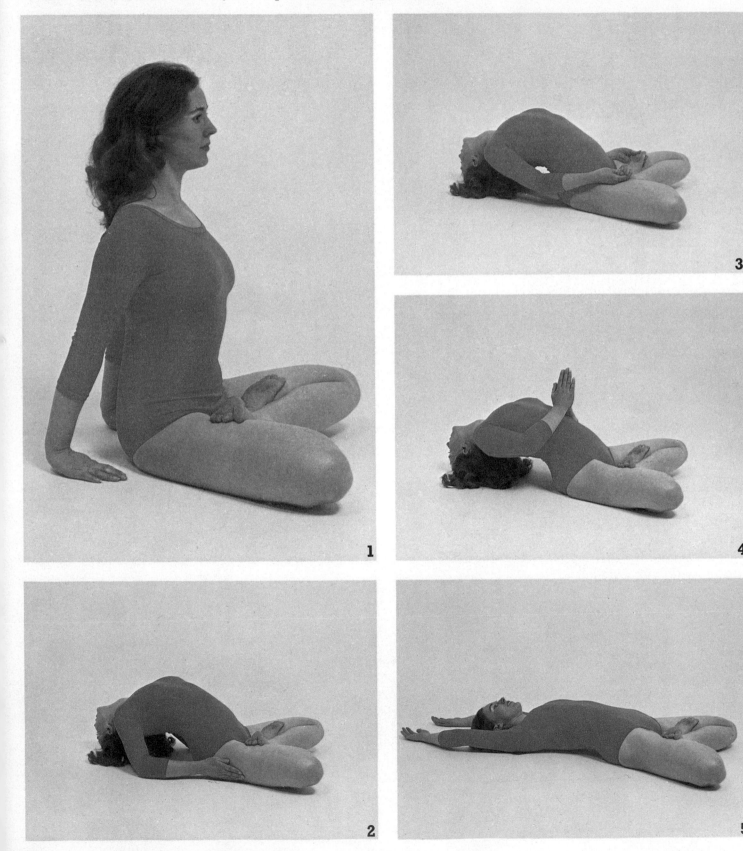

THE FULL LOCUST
Flexes the spine, strengthens the arms, massages the kidneys and lumbar region

Lie on your abdomen with your chin on the floor (see Lesson 15). Make fists with your hands and place them under your abdomen or thighs. Inhale and exhale twice and then, on the third inhalation, swing your legs up as high as possible with a swift movement, keeping them together and straight. Hold for as long as possible, then exhale and slowly lower your legs and thighs to the floor. Relax.
Repeat only once.

1

SALUTATION POSTURE
Stretches the legs, spine, arms and shoulders, strengthens feet and improves balance

1. Stand with your feet together. Lunge forward onto your right foot, bending your right knee low and keeping your left knee and toes on the floor. Inhale and stretch your arms above your head. Hold for five breaths and then slowly come up. Repeat on the other side.
2. Practise an advanced version with your left knee raised.

THE TRIANGLE—7
Stretches the body, strengthens the legs, improves balance

Stand with your feet wide apart. Inhale. Exhale and bend your left knee. Place your left palm behind your left foot and stretch your right arm upwards. Hold for ten. Slowly come up. Repeat to the right.

About the author...

The London School of Yoga overlooks Streatham Common in South London. It is the home and workplace of Lilian K. Donat, author of *Unisex Yoga*, as well as several other books. She has said that yoga is central to her life, and the house, with its serene, peaceful atmosphere is a reflection of this. She is an extraordinarily active person. A prolific writer on various subjects including cooking, plant care, needlework, and also a fine translation of a book on Tantric yoga, she manages to unite both a practical and a highly sensitive approach to life.

Her transition from being very interested in yoga to becoming a yoga teacher in her own right took some time. About six years ago she went to India, and studied under the yoga master Swami Satyananda. When she returned to England, she was visited by a constant flow of swamis, who eventually encouraged her to become a teacher in her own right. The school is still a centre for visiting swamis from all over the world, and naturally, it is a focus for anyone who is interested in yoga, and wishes to meet and talk to them.

As a teacher she is genuinely interested in her students' development, while at the same time, she encourages them to be independent. One, an art teacher, has made some beautiful designs for the yoga room. A large mandala, composed of glowing circles of colour is particularly striking; he painted this after an experience during meditation.

A brilliant teacher, tolerant and encouraging, Lilian Donat lives at the centre of her world, finding yoga limitless in its potential for herself and for the students who come to learn from her.